UNHEARD ECHOES

Modern Family Dynamics Unveiled

By

Alexanderina Tasnadi

DEDICATION

To my beloved children Sean and Sophia...

with love...

Contents

Prologue

This is Maria's story, a resilient survivor from New York City, who overcame a childhood marked by her mother's schizophrenia, abuse, foster care, and separation from her siblings, showcasing her incredible strength and determination.

This book aims to spark change in you, inspiring you to make a positive difference in your community. It sheds light on the struggles of mental health issues, drug use, the foster care system, and child abuse.

For the author, this book hopes to serve as a catalyst for change by encouraging readers to learn from Maria's story and help create a better future for those in need. While the names have been changed to protect identities, the story recounts true events from Maria's life that have impacted the author.

1

———

It was 1975 and the song "Kung Fu Fighting" by Carlton Douglas was playing on the kitchen radio. My cousin Paula and I were karate chopping and kicking the wall in my grandmother's apartment.

"They are coming to get me! Help me, the birds are coming for me!" She ran into the apartment. I heard my mother screaming.

She kept saying that the birds were going to get her and she jumped inside the bathtub and kept on screaming, "They're coming to get me!!!"

The men came with a stretcher and hauled my mother off to the hospital. My grandmother (who I called Nagymama in Hungarian) told me she was sick, though I saw no injuries. I lived with my mother Lilly, sister Sarah, and Nagymama Ilona in her small one-bedroom apartment on East 96th Street in New York City. Our home faced the busy street and contained just one bedroom that we all shared.

Nagymama's apartment was especially cramped, and the rats that lived there were enormous. The building's garbage cans sat right outside the bedroom windows, drawing swarms of rats into the small home on a regular basis. I was five years old at the time, while my sister Sarah was only two. We split our time between Nagymama's apartment and our mother's even smaller residence in one of Brooklyn's oldest and most run-down public housing complexes in Williamsburg. My mother's apartment had two bedrooms and a separate living room and kitchen. The apartment was much bigger and we were more comfortable but it was dangerous and there was never any heat or hot water.

I visited my mother in the hospital for the first time that I can remember. There, I met a kind Spanish lady named Angela who said she was my grandmother. She gave Sarah and me each a big box with a fancy bow and a small bottle of perfume tied to the ribbon. Inside the box was a fancy dress, like the ones we wore to church. Angela said she loved my mom, but I didn't know why, as I didn't remember ever seeing her before.

My mom was happy to see Sarah. She kissed and held her, but when I said hello, she didn't even look at me. What did I do wrong? She always played with my younger sister and tickled her, but she told me I was too big. We went home, and across the street lived my Nagypapa Jullian. He had a green Cadillac, and I loved it when he took me for rides around the block. My Nagypapa was a classical violinist. He would play for me and my dolls, especially at bedtime.

Once, I stayed over at Nagypapa's apartment with my step-grandmother Anny. She would make hot chocolate while Nagypapa played the violin for me and my dolls at bedtime. Sometimes, Nagypapa took me to the Hungarian bakery between 1st Avenue and York on 82nd Street to buy all kinds of pastries. On the corner was the Hungarian butcher shop, Tibor Meats. Neither of these wonderful shops is open today. Nagypapa usually bought meat and pastries before dropping me off, always checking to see if we needed anything. I never realized how much he helped us as a kid, but he did his best whenever he could.

My cousin Paula lived on the same block as my grandparents on East 96th Street. I remember her building had stairs that were spiral and narrow and I almost always fell down. My aunt Paula and my cousin Paula, along with my other cousin Charlie (Paula's brother), were a lot of fun to be around. Us kids played hide and seek or *'Ring Around the Rosie'* inside the apartment. If it was nice out, then we would go to the park. The park was only a block away and it had swings and a see-saw.

My Aunt Paula was younger than my mom, only 20 years old. She had my cousin Paula when she was just 14 and Charlie at 15. She was a tough cookie, often speaking in a loud or angry tone. Despite this, she was always kind and sweet to me and my Nagymama.

Aunt Paula had a boyfriend, Earl who was an African American. He wasn't the father of my cousins. I remember Earl was tall, with a big afro, and lived with my Aunt Paula. He kept a sawed-off shotgun hidden under the sofa in the living room. Earl sold drugs to people driving towards the FDR Drive in NYC, and his territory included a nearby park. My mom and aunt often smoked pot together, and I remember seeing Aunt Paula sniffing glue from a bag to get high. Most of the time, though, they stuck to smoking pot.

My Nagymama hated me going over to Aunt Paula's apartment with my mother because she knew it was to buy drugs and get high. Aunt Paula had two brothers, Chris and Emmeral, who was named after their father. Chris, the younger brother, was fun and would always dance with me and my cousins. We listened to a lot of soul music and rhythm and blues. At that time, we were listening to Marvin Gaye's *Mercy Mercy Me*, and *What's Going On* from The Ecology album 1971. There was a song called *The Bottle* sung by Gil Scott-Heron. It was about an alcoholic man. However, my mom said it was my sister's song because she wouldn't leave her baby bottle.

Sarah wouldn't stop drinking from her baby bottle, and it was ruining her front teeth. My mom joked that it was her "song" because of the rhythm it made. I enjoyed it because it gave me a good beat to dance to. I loved dancing as a kid, and my Uncle Chris was an amazing dancer. He would come over to my Nagymama's apartment and sleep on the cot we had in the kitchen whenever he stayed late. Uncle Chris was always dancing or playing games with us kids. He was great, especially when Nagymama asked him to set the rat traps. I would laugh every time the trap snapped, but he never got angry. He was my favorite uncle.

When I was around six, my mother decided we would move into the Brooklyn apartment permanently. My Nagymama gave up her apartment on East 96th Street and moved in with us to Williamsburg, Brooklyn. It was 1976 and we were listening to Stevie Wonder's album *Songs In The Key of Life*. Little did I know the impact the album would have on me as I got older. My mother's favorite song from the album was *'Ngiculela,'* a beautiful blend of African and Spanish lyrics. It was a love song, and I can still remember her voice when she sang it. She loved to sing and often locked herself in the living room to listen to music and get high.

I used to go into the living room and dance to the music that was playing like Carlos Santana's Abraxas album. It had the hit songs *Black Magic Woman*, and *Oye Como Va* but my favorite song was *Se A Cabo*. I loved this music to dance to as a kid. It was a lot of fun twirling in the living room and my mom whipping her head from side to side. The living room was always filled with smoke from mom's cigarettes and pot. Nagymama would yell at her to turn down the music and keep us kids out of the room when she was smoking. We didn't understand why at the time; we just knew it was bad because we were told it was.

This was still a happy time for us because we were still all together with our biological family. I would wake up and go to the kitchen and my Nagymama would be sitting at the kitchen table. She always had a cigarette in one hand and a cup of coffee in the other with a big smile and a hug for us always. My Nagymama would always shower us with kisses in the morning and ask us what we wanted for breakfast.

Sometimes, when we received food stamps, she would buy kielbasa sausage and cook it for breakfast with peppers, tomatoes, onions, and plenty of paprika. It was my favorite, even over eggs. We'd also have it with stone bread that Nagymama baked herself. She made almost all our bread and pastries.

Each morning, we'd wake up, and Nagymama would heat water on the stove because we didn't have hot water. She'd pour it into the bathroom sink with a stopper, where I'd use it to wash my face. After washing up, we always said our prayers.

We are Roman Catholic. My Nagymama was very religious and made us pray in the morning and at night. We also went to church every morning. I went to mass every day before school and after mass, my Nagymama would take me to the store to buy chocolate coins, and maybe a bag of chips. She gave me 35 cents for snacks every day for school.

After buying my chocolates, she'd take Sarah and me to the park across the street from school. If we had time, she'd put us on the swings before school started. The schoolyard was just across the street, and we could see and hear the bell when it was time to go in. I loved going to school because it was warm in the winter, and we got breakfast and lunch there when we ran out of food.

Running out of food and eating in school was a regular thing for most of us kids in the family. It seemed that it was also that way for many of the kids in my school. I would go to the free breakfast line and it would be full of kids. I didn't mind eating in school because I would be able to go and play and make friends. I did however not like it when Sarah and I would go to our friends' house to eat.

We had a neighbor on the first floor named Maritza. She and her husband, David, were Puerto Rican. They had a son, David Jr., who was a year older than me, and a daughter, Lizette, who was the same age as Sarah. Maritza was always kind to us, frequently giving us clothes from her nieces. When her twin nieces outgrew their clothes, she collected them for me.

Maritza was great. She was always feeding us whenever she had extra but I didn't like eating at her apartment. Her husband David would always pretend that he was playing with me or picking me up like his daughter Lizette. David was not playing with me; he was always touching me and putting his hands up my dress. Maritza and David had a house in Puerto Rico and they used to visit there every summer. When they came back, they brought back a hand-churning coffee grinder. Maritza gave it to me and told her husband David to show me how to use it. He put coffee beans inside and showed me how to turn the handle to grind the coffee.

When Maritza walked out of the room, he put his hand up against my vagina. I wanted to fight back, but I felt powerless. I tried to tell my Nagymama, but she dismissed it as if I was lying or it was my fault. So, I did my best to avoid him, pretending I wasn't hungry. Whenever we played hide and seek or tag in their apartment, I made sure to leave before the dad got home.

Otherwise, we would go to the playground together to have fun on the slides and merry-go-rounds. The project had water sprinklers shaped like ocean animals—whales, dolphins, and sharks. During the summer, you'd find us there, along with Jane, Angie, and Susie, Bell's daughters from the apartment downstairs.

My mother became friends with Bell, an African American woman with a charming Southern accent. I always thought her accent was cute. Bell had a white rabbit named Trixie, which she bought for her daughters. My sister and I loved going downstairs to play with Trixie. Looking back, those moments were some of the happiest times in my life.

2

───────

It's now 1977 and my *Happy Birthday* sign was up on the kitchen wall above my Nagymama and we were going to have my party. Nagymama was ordering a birthday cake with cherry filling. I was excited because my babysitter Isabella, along with her mother and friends, were coming over. My friends from downstairs and my cousins were also coming. My cousins are my first cousins because their mother and my mother are sisters. I'm named after my Aunt Maria, while my cousin Lilly is named after my mother. My aunt also has a daughter named Elisabeth and a son named Luis Jr.

Everyone arrived, and I was thrilled. I wanted everyone to meet my friend Susie, who was in my class that year and also a neighbor. My cousin Lily, as always, was friendly and started dancing with Susie. Sarah was being tickled by Isabella and then she saw me come into the room with Susie. Isabella told me to stay away from that *'dirty thing,'* so I looked around to see what was dirty so I wouldn't ruin my party dress. Then she told me, "Maria, you can't be friends with that dirty black girl."

"She's not dirty and she's my friend here and in school," I told her.

"No... You can't be friends with a nigger..." She said to me.

I didn't know what exactly that was. I just knew that it was something bad because Susie went downstairs crying. I knew that was a bad name to say to African American people but what exactly it meant, I had no clue. I was just turning seven years old. My mom called me and it was time to cut the cake and everyone was there, singing *Happy Birthday* except my friend Susie.

The next day, my mom and I were downstairs at Bell's apartment. Bell told my mother what Isabella said about Susie. Now that made my mother furious. My mother yelled at me. I came out of Susie's room and went into the living room where my mom and Bell were. My mother gave me a hard slap and I fell and started crying. I had no idea why she hit me. She told me how dare I call Susie a nigger. I told her I didn't, and that it was Isabella. I tried to tell them Susie was my friend and how much I cared about her. But she said I couldn't be her friend. At that moment, Bell yelled at mom and told her that I tried to defend Susie but her friend and my babysitter Isabella wouldn't let me defend her daughter.

"It's your friend's fault, not Maria's," Bell said to my mother.

Mum said to me 'it better be her.' However, she didn't even say sorry to me for hitting me.

Religion was a big deal in my house. We did not eat meat on Fridays at all the entire year-round. My Nagymama thought it was time for me to begin my catechism classes. So, I went to class for the first time at our local church on Saturday afternoon. My Nagymama forgot the time to pick me up so the Nun asked me if I knew the way home. I said yes and she walked me home. She was very nice and sweet.

When I got home, mom asked me what we did in class that day. I showed her the picture of the church I made. My mother asked me if they explained the three different spiritual levels. I said I don't know.

She then explained about the Virgin Mary and that she stays

in a place called Purgatory for the sinners who are waiting to go to heaven.

"It's where sinners wait between Heaven and Hell until their sins are forgiven. People pray for them so they can eventually go to Heaven," she said.

She continued, "Hell is for people who the Devil is waiting for because they have killed people or their souls are bad and have to go back to Hell. Heaven is for angels and people who don't sin or who are very good like your Nagymama."

She asked if I remembered the picture in my baby album. I mentioned the one where I was just born, with my head shaved, wires attached, and a tube in my mouth.

My mother said, "That's the one. You were born very sick, you almost died."

"Remember I told you that before so you would know why they put the wires on your head and tubes in your mouth. I took pictures of you because I thought you were going to die. You were not supposed to live. You were supposed to die and go back to Hell with the Devil. It's not your fault but you have to go back to where you belong with the Devil. You can't do anything bad because your Nagymama takes you to church every day. Every day you put holy water on yourself inside the church every morning before you go to school. Because you go to church every day and you pray day and night you have been able to keep the Devil away, but not for long. I see you when you're sleeping. You're losing all the goodness in you and the evil in you is growing."

"But mom... I didn't do anything bad," I cried.

She told me it wasn't my fault, but that I was born with a

bad soul. I was terrified and didn't know what to think. When I told my Nagymama what my mother said, they had a huge argument. My mother ended up throwing both of us out. She kept Sarah with her.

Nagymama and I went to her sister Judith's apartment in New York City. We took the subway. I remember we used to take the LL to 14th Street then you have to take the shuttle train to the East or West side of NYC. The LL doesn't exist, it's just the L now but it still goes to Graham Ave in Brooklyn.

I loved Aunt Judith. She was always happy to see us. Whenever we went over, we saw Uncle Chris, Uncle Emmeral, Aunt Paula and her kids and Aunt Judy who is Aunt Judith's daughter also and she has four children Karen, Melissa, Liza, and Johnny. We got there at night time and it was cold. Nagymama made hot cocoa and biscuits with lots of butter and I watched Sesame Street.

Aunt Judith got home from work. I ran over and gave her a kiss. She asked what happened and why wasn't my mom and Sarah with us. So, my Nagymama explained to her that my mom thinks 'I have to go back to Hell because I belong to the Devil.' She just looked at me and said, "Don't worry, you can stay as long as you like. Your poor mother is crazy. Don't believe anything she says because she is very sick in the head."

I asked her if it was like a headache.

"No sweetheart... Your mother is crazy. She has schizophrenia. It's a type of sickness in the brain that makes people crazy. Your mother isn't taking her medication so she's not thinking right."

"So, I don't have the Devil in me?" I asked, to which Nagymama and Aunt Judith both said, "No! That's your crazy mother saying crazy things. Don't believe her."

The next day, we all went out to the Hungarian bakery on 82nd Street and we bumped into some old friends of Nagymama from back in Hungary before she and my mother came to this country: two sisters, Anna and Klara. They both had daughters the same age and they were both ballerinas. Anna's daughter, Agota, and Klara's daughter, Viktoria, danced so beautifully. I loved watching them leap into the air and perform their pirouettes.

I wanted to be a ballerina. Ballerinas were so graceful and danced so elegantly. I used to watch them do their warm-ups and their splits. I thought they were amazing whenever they finished doing an entire dance practice with the twirling and leaps. My Nagymama and Aunt Judith invited Anna and Klara back to my aunt's apartment for coffee. The grownups were talking and then they asked me if I wanted to go to Anna's house. I of course said yes. I loved the idea of being with Agota and having her teach me ballet.

Nagymama and I went to Anna's house. It was a big building with two apartments but they kept the third-floor apartment empty. They lived on the second floor, above a store. When we arrived, Anna was there and she had another daughter named after her little Anna. She wasn't little, she was special and she had a brother Janos named after the father and her brother was also special. My Nagymama told me that Janos Jr. and Little Anna were both mentally retarded. For this reason, they are not like their sister Agota (the ballerina) and we should show them more love and kindness.

"That's what God would want us to do, Maria. Can you do that for me? Be extra kind and loving to special people?" Nagymama asked me.

I told her 'Yes,' because I always wanted to make her and God happy. When Agota came home from dance school, I gave her a big hug and asked if I could sleep with her later. She said yes, and I also asked if she would paint my nails like hers, just like the big girls do. She agreed. I loved Agota because she was always kind and played with me. As she practiced a routine for her Chicago Ballet tryout, I quietly moved to the back of the living room so I wouldn't get in her way. I tried to do her warm-ups like bending and stretching and doing a side split and the Russian split. I tried standing on my toes like Agota. Agota told me I was doing very well.

Suddenly, two boys showed up. Agota introduced them as her cousins: Tommy, who was thirteen, and Luke, who was seven like me. They went up to the apartment on the third floor. Curious, I asked Agota why they were going up there. She explained that their father was up there, giving them piano lessons. A piano is what they were learning from their father. So, I asked, why aren't they learning to play the violin?

"My Nagypapa plays the violin like your dad and he's their uncle so he can teach them to play the violin. My cousin Luis is learning to play the violin from my Nagypapa and he's five years old," I told her.

Agota said it was up to the dad and not up to the boys on what instrument they were going to learn to play.

I heard someone play the piano. It must have been the dad because it sounded so pretty like classical music. It sounded like the kind of music I was used to hearing from my Nagypapa playing by Johann Sebastian Bach. Curious to see who was playing, I decided to go upstairs and take a peek. I got to the third floor and when you first opened the door, it led you into a long hallway. Then there was a kitchen, and the living room, and in the back was another big room with the piano and the boys and the dad.

The big boy Tommy was playing the piano. It sounded so polished and mature, like an adult was playing. How can he play the piano so well? I'm going to tell my Nagymama. I went downstairs and I told her that it was Tommy playing the piano so pretty. Nagymama smiled and said, 'he's going to be your husband when you grow up and Luke is going to be Sarah's husband when she grows up.'

"Yuk! Why??? I don't need a husband. I'm going to be a ballerina like Agota," I said loudly. Everyone just looked at me and laughed. Agota said after she becomes a famous ballerina, she's going to get married. Everyone gets married eventually.

"I don't want to be married. My Nagymama is not married and my mom is not married..." Oh God, I was so naïve back then.

That evening, I went to the bedroom with Agota and I was sitting on the edge of the bed. I had my hands open with my fingers spread out so Agota could paint my nails.

"What color are you going to paint them?" I asked.

"Clear with sparkles, like a princess," she said.

"Oh my... really???" I was excited. That's why I loved Agota, she always made me happy. I was blowing on my nails to dry. She said 'they are dry, and now it's time for sleep.' So, I said my prayers and went to sleep.

The next morning, when I woke up, Nagymama brought my clothes and towels into the room and took me to the bathroom for a bath. There was a knock on the door.

Nagymama said we were in there, but it wasn't the boys—it was my mother. Nagymama opened the door and told her she was giving me a bath. My mom looked at me and said 'who told you that you can have nail polish on and you didn't sleep with Nagymama?'

'How did she know?' She hit me on my butt and kept on hitting me. Nagymama told her to stop saying that we were in someone else's house and they didn't need to know our problems. Nagymama finished giving me a bath and dressed me. I went downstairs to eat some toast and cocoa and Agota was there talking to my mom.

"I told you, your daughter Maria had a lot of fun with me last night. Didn't you Maria?" She looked at me and asked.

I had said yes but she saw that I had been crying. She also saw that my thigh was red, the part of that dress that wasn't covering me when I sat on the chair. Her mother Anna asked 'what happened?' I didn't say anything because I knew mom was going to hit me again.

Nagymama said, "Sorry Anna, we haven't been honest with you this time around. We have been staying away from my daughter because she keeps hitting Maria. She is not taking her medications and insists that there is something wrong or evil with Maria. Maria is seven years old, I take her to church, and to school. She is so well-behaved. What on earth could be wrong with her?"

My mother started yelling, "You don't understand. She was born very sick, and she almost died. She was supposed to die."

"So, what are you going to do, kill her? Are you completely crazy?" Anna asked.

"No, I'm not going to kill her, but I'm not going to let her stray from the path of righteousness. Even if I have to beat her every day," mom shouted.

Nagymama said, "Then just give her up to me. You're not going to beat this child every day of her life. Just give her to me, I'll raise her and you can keep Sarah. You only show attention to Sarah."

Anna also said to my mom, "Let your mother raise Maria. Your mother could move in here upstairs and raise Maria here. Maria can go to school with Luke."

My mom ran out and left Sarah behind. That night, Nagymama started to worry and called my Aunt Maria, my mother's sister. She hoped Maria might have heard from mom or seen her. Maria said she hadn't. Nagymama then called Aunt Judith to check if mom had been in touch. Judith mentioned that she had told mom where we were last night, but she hadn't heard from her today. My grandmother was crying, and everyone was trying to tell her that things would work out.

We all were in a state of total chaos. Anna was teaching me and Sarah a Hungarian nursery rhythm song about a squirrel when the phone rang. It was from the hospital. The doctor said my mother had voluntarily admitted herself to the psychiatric ward of the hospital. Anna told that to Nagymama and she was not worried anymore.

They both told me that my mommy didn't mean to hit me or say those bad things about me. She's just very sick in the head. She's now in the hospital and the doctors are going to make her better.

The next day, Sarah and I were playing hide and seek with

Tommy, Luke, Anna, and Janos upstairs and we were playing house with our dolls. Later, we went downstairs to have lunch and then went back upstairs to watch TV. We were watching *'Bozo the Clown.'* I loved the show because Bozo called you up by your name. Then he wrote your name and made a picture out of the letters of your name. There was a boy named Jeff and he made an elephant out of his name, so I thought it was great.

We went to play hide and seek again. This time Tommy followed me and said we were playing in teams, I said 'Okay.' He followed me into the closet. I told him to hide somewhere else. He said no and pushed me to the floor and kissed me on the mouth. I pushed him away but he was too heavy. He put his tongue in my mouth and wouldn't stop. I started to cry and he called me a baby.

I went to Little Anna and Janos and told them what he did. He said I was lying so I told Nagymama but he denied it again. She told me to not play alone with the boys because they are fresh. The next day, we went home back to Brooklyn.

It was the evening and the phone rang, so Nagymama said 'go get it.' I answered and it was mom. She asked what I was doing. I told her I was watching *Jaws* with Sarah and Nagymama. She told me to not scare Sarah. I told her I didn't, but she wouldn't believe me. My mom then told me that she's better and the doctors are going to let her come home tomorrow.

I was scared and didn't know what to do. My mother asked me to speak to my grandmother, so I handed her the phone. I heard their conversation and made out that mom was coming home. Sarah was thrilled, of course—my mother never hit her or threatened her. I asked Nagymama what Mom had said on the phone.

"Don't worry... As long as she takes her medicine, she won't hit you and I won't leave you alone with her I promise," she hugged me and told me.

Mom came home two days later. It was July 13th,1977 and there was a blackout in New York City. We had to keep our doors locked because people were going around stealing and looting throughout the city. The police were shooting and people were running down the street with radios and TVs. I saw them through my second-floor window facing the street.

Nagymama said to stay away from the window because of the shooting. Sarah and I hid underneath our beds. We had two twin beds that Nagymama pushed together so that Sarah, Nagymama, and I could all sleep together. My mom slept in the other bedroom. She had a big queen size bed all to herself. At night, she came into the room and told us not to be scared. We fell asleep and the next day, the lights were back on. I turned on the TV and they were showing all the stores that had been broken into and the property damages that happened the night before.

It was weird because the day before, my mom took me to New York Eye and Ear Hospital on 14th Street New York City. I used to go there for eye therapy because I have what the doctor said is a lazy eye. That's why my eye is a little crossed and I don't see well in the right eye. I only see with my left eye. I really liked eye therapy because they turned the lights off and I played with a toy called Light-Brite. It had colored light bulbs that lit up when I put them inside the lite up canvas. We couldn't afford that toy so I got to play with it when I did my eye exercises.

The only thing that was frustrating during therapy was that I had to wear a patch over my right eye. So, I couldn't see anything! It made doing the shape more difficult because I couldn't see the outline. I liked the doctor who tried showing me how to do the outline even though I couldn't see. He was very nice. He told my mom I had to do exercises at home with a patch on my eye every day for an hour. So, my Nagymama tried to have me sew or follow a handkerchief design with needle and thread, while wearing my eye patch. My mom was really nice to me when we would go to the eye doctor. She would buy me popcorn on the way there and she wasn't mean anymore.

Then one day, I was trying to sew a handkerchief at the kitchen table. I sat in the middle chair, while Nagymama sat by the stove, which was under the window. She always took that spot because she did all the cooking. My mom was on my right side. Suddenly, mom asked me why I was sewing it wrong on purpose. I told her I wasn't. She insisted I was doing it intentionally because I was making signs for the Devil. I was terrified; I knew my mom was sick again.

"Do not look at your grandmother or I will kill you. Stop sewing signs to the Devil or I will burn you with this cigarette." She put the cigarette that she had in her hand closer to my leg and I started to cry. Nagymama asked what was wrong, and why was I crying. I jumped off the chair because she tried to burn me with her cigarette.

Nagymama called Aunt Maria and asked if we could come to stay with her because Mom wasn't well and was causing trouble again. Aunt Maria said she couldn't take us in because she and Uncle Luis were fighting, and she planned to come over to our apartment instead. Nagymama suggested that maybe things would improve if Aunt Maria was here.

Later on, that night, Aunt Maria came banging at our door

with my cousins screaming 'HELP!' Nagymama opened the door and everyone tried to close the door before Uncle Luis could get in. The door was closing on his fingers and he was screaming. Everyone in the building opened their doors and told him to stop and leave. They were calling the police on uncle Luis.

Bell and Maritza were used to uncle Luis fighting and causing problems. It wasn't the first time they had to call the police. My grandmother opened the door just enough to let his fingers lose and then we locked the door with the steel bolt. Now my cousins were over with Aunt Maria. She was crying to Nagymama.

"He just wouldn't stop beating little Luis. He was punching him like a grown man; he was only five years old. Then he grabbed my hair and threw me against the wall and threw furniture at me," she told Nagymama.

"Later, he locked me up in the bathroom. He sat me on the toilet and chained me up and started to stab me in my thighs with a small knife. When he left, I yelled for the kids to help me get the chains off so we could get out of the house before their father came back. I grabbed a bag and put diapers inside for Ingrid (the baby they just had a few months ago)," she was continuously crying.

Now that my cousins were here, we would have fun playing at night together. Sarah and I went into our drawers and looked for our pajamas so we could lend them to our cousins because Aunt Maria showed up without any clothes.

Aunt Maria was very pretty. She had long, jet-black hair that reached down to her waist, full eyelashes that nearly touched her eyebrows, and heart-shaped lips.

I often wondered why Aunt Maria, who was so beautiful, had ended up with someone like Uncle Luis. All he seemed to do was make her cry. My cousins and I were all afraid of him. Even though he never hit me, he scared me. He was always shouting, slamming doors, and throwing furniture when he drank. He would get so drunk that he would toss plates and cups around, making everyone uneasy.

Whenever the holidays came around, Uncle Luis would start by drinking and getting drunk. When he was really intoxicated, he would hit the kids and Aunt Maria. One day, I asked Nagymama why I didn't have a daddy. She explained that my father had acted the same way towards my mother as Uncle Luis did towards Aunt Maria. He would hit my mother when he was drunk, which led to their divorce. That's why I didn't have a father.

I couldn't understand why the men in our family always hit the women and the children. All of my uncles, even my grandpa, were known for this. I had heard stories about how he used to hit my grandma. Why did they do this? My father and uncles were Puerto Rican, while my mother was Hungarian. Unfortunately, my grandparents on my mother's side had a deep-seated prejudice against Puerto Ricans. They believed that Puerto Rican men only knew how to drink, get drunk, and abuse women and children.

This isn't always the case, but it seemed to be true in my family. The men in my family had proven this theory correct— drinking, becoming abusive, and violent. It was a painful stereotype that we lived with. Yet, our neighbor downstairs, Maritza, and her husband are Puerto Rican, and they are nothing like that. My grandmother liked them very much, and my mom was friends with them. They were good people who worked hard. The husband didn't drink and never hurt his family. Seeing them, I knew it wasn't true that all Puerto Ricans were abusive towards their wives or children.

I asked my Aunt Maria if it was true that my Daddy hit my mommy.

"Sweety, your dad kicked your mommy in the belly when she was pregnant with your sister Sarah. He dragged her down the stairs in the building by her hair and he was punching and kicking her all the way into the street and that's why they got a divorce," she said.

With Aunt Maria and my cousins here, I no longer had to fear my mom. While Aunt Maria was around, she made sure my mom didn't hurt me. My cousins and I had a lot of fun playing together.

After a few days, Uncle Luis returned and apologized for his behavior. As usual, Aunt Maria and Uncle Luis made up, and he took us all to McDonald's. Then he drove my grandmother, Sarah, and me back home. However, Aunt Maria and my cousin stayed behind to return with him to their house in the Bronx.

3

The next day, I had school and my mother picked me up because it was Wednesday and I had a half a day so I went to New York Eye and Ear Hospital for my eye therapy in New York City on 14th Street. On the way home, my mother asked me what I was doing at night. I was confused and asked her what she meant.

"What were you doing at night?" She asked me again.

"I don't understand Mom, what are you asking?"

"Are you doing your prayers the right way?" She inquired.

"Yes, I'm still saying my prayers every night with Sarah in front of Nagymama." I felt a pang of fear when she asked if I was doing my prayers correctly. I knew something was wrong but couldn't figure out what. After that, she didn't ask me anything more. When we got home, she made tea with various herbs and asked me to take a bath. She gave Sarah and me both a bath before serving us the tea.

When we finished taking a bath, she poured the specialty tea that cooled off on top of us but we cannot dry off this special tea. She said the specialty tea was to ward off bad spirits. Then she lit up these special candles that had pictures of the saints on them. After that, we have to say our prayers to the Virgin Mary. We have to say the rosary because she said that there were evil spirits that were trying to attack us.

My mother, my sister, my grandmother, and I all went to Isabella's grandmother's house, whom we called Ma. On her kitchen table, Ma had a crystal ball and used to read tarot cards. She practiced Santería, a religion blending African, Hispanic, and Catholic elements. This faith involves worshiping saints, praying to them, and making offerings like food and money.

Ma asked Sarah and me to place our hands over a clear glass bowl filled with holy water and a camphor tablet. She instructed us to say the Our Father prayer over it. This ritual, she explained, was meant to help drive away the bad spirits that were supposedly surrounding us and troubling our family. According to Ma and Isabella, my mother believed there were supernatural forces at work in our home.

However, I thought there was nothing wrong, only my mom's imagination creating problems.

Ma instructed my mother and grandmother on how to prepare more of the specialty tea. She explained that after it cooled, they should pour it over Sarah and me following our baths for three days. This process was meant to cleanse us and remove any negative energy. Then every night, during our prayers, we also had to ask Saint Michael the Archangel to defend us in the battle against the evil and the wickedness and the snares of the devil because, except my grandmother, they all believed in these supernatural threats.

I asked Nagymama if she thinks there's something that's going on. She said no but if it keeps my mother from hurting me, she doesn't care.

"If this is able to keep her calm and it keeps her from hurting you, I don't mind doing this at all," she said.

The holiday season was here, and we were heading to Aunt Maria's house for Thanksgiving. When we arrived, Uncle Luis was there with his brother and sisters, who had come down from upstate New York. It was a lively gathering with lots of kids my age and my cousins' ages, so there were about 15 of us running around and having a blast.

Even though my mom was having fun because she brought her new boyfriend, Alfredo with her. She had met him at my school, where he worked as a security guard. He even took me to see *Star Wars*, which I thought was the best movie ever. I was fascinated by the robots and wanted them, especially R2-D2 and C-3PO. At that time, I thought the movie was simply amazing. My mom really liked Alfredo because she said he was very good-looking. She said he looked like a Spanish version of Al Pacino and she really liked Al Pacino. I wasn't sure if he resembled Al Pacino; all I knew was that he had a beard, a mustache, and big glasses. I liked him because he brought a big dog to our house. I loved the dog, but we couldn't keep him because he was too big for our apartment.

I also liked him because, at school, he always said hello to me and made sure the other kids didn't pick on me like they used to. He was very kind and bought coats for me and Sarah since we didn't have the money for them. That year, he made sure we had warm coats, and I thought he was very nice. We used to go to his parents' house and his mom would always have Malta in the refrigerator for us to drink and cookies to eat which I really loved eating. They were very nice to us.

The children went to sit in the kitchen dining area for Thanksgiving dinner, while the grown-ups went to the fancy dining room. All of a sudden, I heard glass break and uncle Luis screaming at my mom and aunt Maria saying to my mom, "Are you crazy??? What are you doing?"

Uncle Luis, his sisters, and his brothers were all saying 'don't do that' and everybody yelling at each other. I got up and went into the dining room to see what was going on. Nagymama explained that Mom had thrown a glass of wine at Uncle Luis, and it had shattered. I was sure that Uncle Luis was going to hit Mom for what she had done. Thankfully that didn't happen. Her boyfriend Alfredo had said to her, "Why don't we go home? She said 'Okay, get the kids and their coats on and get them ready.' I didn't want to leave; I wanted to stay and have my Thanksgiving dinner. We took the train home.

As soon as we got home, my mother started making stuffing and she put it inside a chicken and we had chicken and stuffing for Thanksgiving dinner at home. Then, Alfredo finished having dinner with me, my mother, Nagymama, and Sarah and left with my mom. My mom would sometimes go and stay with Alfredo at his house with his parents.

My mom returned shortly after and said she felt I was doing evil things to my sister, Sarah. She couldn't trust me alone with her in the house, especially with sharp objects, so she took all the forks and knives, including the butter knives, and handed them to Maritza for safekeeping.

The next day, my mother locked the door to my bedroom, where Nagymama was sleeping and Sarah was watching TV. She made sure they couldn't get out. Then she set a pot of water on the stove, adding red chili flakes, chili powder, black pepper, and other spices. As the water boiled, she told me to get undressed. I was still wearing my nightgown since it was nighttime. I didn't want to get undressed. I was crying. She said you better take off now! She made me go into the living room. She took a wooden spoon and she brought the pot of boiling water with the spices.

She put me over her knee, picked up the wooden spoon, and dipped it into the boiling water and she beat me on behind with that wooden spoon. I was screaming and crying. In the chaos, I managed to escape and ran out of the apartment, heading downstairs to Maritza's place. I was totally naked but I didn't care. I got away from her. I remember putting my hands over my private parts. Maritza had a house full of people. I was feeling embarrassed but I had to get away from my mom. I was crying. She was yelling for me.

Everyone was outside, even Bell. My grandmother finally managed to get out of the room and promised she would take care of me and stop my mom from hurting me again. I was doubtful because my mother managed to lock her in a room and still found a way to get to me. What could my grandmother do to protect me when my mom was so determined? I was terrified and had no other place to go, so I had to return home. Reluctantly, I went back upstairs, pretending to be asleep while my mom talked to Nagymama. My Nagymama told my mom that 'you can't go around beating a child with a wooden spoon dipped in boiling water. That is torture you cannot do that.'

When Thanksgiving break was over, I returned to school with my grandmother. She accompanied me to the main office and instructed me to translate her message to the office lady. She asked me to explain our situation and seek their help. I detailed the events that had occurred over the Thanksgiving break and what my mother had done to me.

The lady at the school explained that the school can't help and that it's not their problem or their business saying 'you have to take care of what's going on in your home.'

So, Nagymama told me to ask the lady in the school where

we needed to go to ask for help with my mom. She said if she had a problem, we needed to call the hospital because she sounded like she needed help from a doctor. We told her that she's been in the hospital before but they let her come home even if she's not well. The lady said there's nothing they can do. We just looked at each other and we didn't know what to do.

After school, my grandmother picked me up and took me to our local church. We went into the rectory and we explained the same story to the priest asking for help. The priest told us that the only thing he could do for us was say a mass prayer to help us in our time of need but that there was nothing else he could do for us.

It was Christmas time, and the building was filled with the sounds of *Saturday Night Fever*. My mom had recently made a new friend in the building. The lady, Elizabeth, had just moved in with her mother. Elizabeth and my mom hit it off quickly, bonding over a movie outing to see *Saturday Night Fever*. They became good friends and enjoyed spending time together.

When *Saturday Night Fever* came out, everyone was talking about it. My mom was especially taken with the movie and its soundtrack. She bought the record, and we listened to every song on the album all day long. I loved the music too, and I danced to it in the living room. It was a great time.

Christmas was a time that always made my mom very happy. She loved decorating, from stringing lights on the Christmas tree to hanging them in the window for everyone to see. She even arranged lights on the kitchen wall in the shape of a Christmas tree. This year, she seemed especially joyful, as she was engaged to be married to Alfredo.

We went to a party at Isabella's grandmother's house for her

'Sweet Sixteen.' It was a very fancy affair. Alfredo mentioned that Ma was also his grandmother, making Isabella his cousin. I remember thinking it was amazing that we were going to be related to our babysitter. I really liked Isabella; she was funny, with blue eyes and a great sense of humor. She used to tickle us a lot and always made things fun. They had a lot of fancy foods and decorations for her Sweet 16. I remember thinking, as I looked around, that I hoped I could have a Sweet Sixteen party just like Isabella's when I turned 16.

My mom was very embarrassed. She wanted to dance with Alfredo but he didn't want to dance and she kept asking him in front of everyone. I felt so embarrassed. Alfredo didn't like to dance. He wasn't like uncle Chris who loved to dance. Soon, they cut the cake and the party was over and we went home and we got party favors that you wear called capias and I remember thinking they were so pretty to wear. It had a ribbon with your name on it and the date and the event and it had a flower attached to it as well. They were pretty.

My mom was pregnant, and we were excited, especially since we thought it might be a boy. But she kept insisting that I was being evil again. My grandmother took me to make a phone call outside the house so that my mom wouldn't listen in on the conversation. We called Aunt Maria, and my grandmother convinced her to let me, my sister, and my grandmother stay at her house because my mom was becoming uncontrollable. She wanted to hit me again and do the special tea baths and candle rituals with the saints on them. My mom even told my grandmother that she wanted to perform an exorcism, believing I was possessed by the Devil. After hearing this, Aunt Maria agreed and told us to bring our clothes.

Aunt Maria enrolled me in school, and I went to classes with my cousins. For a while, it was great—I didn't have to worry about my mom hitting me. However, the fighting between Uncle Luis and Aunt Maria was escalating, and it was becoming really difficult to ignore. So, one day we all went to Aunt Judith's apartment. We were cramped but we didn't have to worry about Uncle Luis beating Aunt Maria and my mom torturing me.

I hated my life, I felt scared all the time and it was cold and there wasn't enough food for all of us kids. I didn't have shoes that fit properly—there were holes in the soles, and they were so tight they were rubbing the skin off my feet. Despite this, we were safe at Aunt Maria's apartment. She promised she would start looking for a place of our own.

A couple of days later, Aunt Maria told us she couldn't find an affordable apartment that would fit all of us. She was in tears, feeling helpless. Uncle Luis showed up and apologized once more, and Aunt Maria decided to return home. This time, we couldn't go with her; my mom threatened to call the police on Aunt Maria if we stayed. So, my Nagymama took Sarah and me back to our mother.

The day after we arrived back in Brooklyn, my mother started with the special prayers again and the special baths with candles that had pictures of the saints on them to get rid of the evil spirits. All of a sudden, my mom wakes me up at night.

"Get up, get dressed now!"

Nagymama said, "what are you doing in the middle of the night?"

"Oh no... You don't understand... This Devil worshiper is going to kill us all. One of the candles that had Jesus Christ's picture on it just broke all by itself while it was burning. I know it was this one's fault, this Devil worshiper. I'm going to take her to the hospital, maybe they can help her. Help protect us from her," mum kept saying.

My grandmother said I wasn't going anywhere without her. So, we all got dressed in the middle of the night and took the train to New York City. We got to the hospital and my mom told them that I tried to kill them with the knives in the house. The doctor asked me if this was true and I told him 'No.' I told him my mom was crazy but he wouldn't believe me. They admitted me to the hospital. They took my blood sample and they made me stay there in a regular hospital pediatrics room for the night.

4

I woke up to find a tray with cereal, milk, and fruit waiting for me. After breakfast, they told me I had to go to a new place. It was a special home for kids where they shared rooms, went to school during the day, played games, and ate with other kids when they came back. I figured it might not be so bad. I knew I was stuck here, but perhaps it wouldn't be as terrible as I feared.

So, they took me to the elevator and we went to another floor. We walked to this large door that was locked. You have to wait until they unlock the door to get in or out. It's a big steel door and it was only in or out of this unit. They told me that this is the Children's Psychiatric unit. This is where you will talk to the doctor about your feelings, good or bad.

I told the nurse, "I'm not the one that is crazy, it's my mother. She invents things and she likes to beat me and say I'm possessed with the devil."

The nurse looked at me with this odd-looking expression. Then she asked me, "Your mom says you're possessed by the devil?"

"Yeah," I said, "that's why I'm here. She lied and made up a story that I was hurting everyone in the house. The truth is, I never hurt anyone—except for the cockroaches. Those I step on because they are nasty."

My mom has been to this hospital lots of times. She stays here sometimes until the medical insurance won't pay anymore. Sometimes she stays for like two or three months. Someone came and unlocked the big steel door.

The nurse gave them my paperwork and told me the other nurse's name. Then she left and I felt like I was being punished for something I didn't do. I was scared. There were a lot of older kids. Like really big high school kids. The nurse introduced me to my new roommate, Virginia. She had a very short haircut, almost like a boy's, which I'd never seen on a girl before.

Virginia was friendly and showed me the routine. In the morning, I had to make my bed and keep it neat for the day before heading to the lunchroom. The lunchroom had round, colorful tables, and you needed to line up at the window to get your tray of food.

I sat next to Virginia for breakfast, and soon another girl joined us. Her name was Beverly, and she seemed nice. Then there was Sally, who reminded me a bit of my sister Sarah. She was small like Sarah and always cried. I felt like crying too but my Nagymama wasn't there for me and there wasn't anybody else that cared about me.

Doctors and the nurses believed my mom when she was lying about me and when she made up things about me like she told them that I was going to hurt my sister and that she was afraid I might harm everyone with knives, so she gave them to our neighbor Maritza.

The only people who believed me were my Nagymama and Aunt Maria. Aunt Maria wanted to help, but she didn't have the money or authority. She said she wasn't the boss of us kids and that it was our mom. She explained that she'd need to go to court to gain custody of me and Sarah, so we wouldn't have to return to living with Mom on her terms.

My Nagymama believed me too, but she couldn't do much because she didn't have the means to support us independently. She echoed Aunt Maria's sentiment, saying she wasn't in a position to make decisions for us and would need to go to court to seek custody of me and Sarah.

Why did we need a boss? I just wanted to stay living with my Nagymama at Anna's house with Agota. Then I could become a ballerina and we would all be happy. Now, I have strangers bossing me around. I don't know these people and I'm lonely. I wanted to go home. It's scary here with the big kids. They yell a lot and fight even more. There are these huge, intimidating men around, and when the big kids fight, they put the kids in a room at the end of the hall. The room has no bed, no lights, no toilet—nothing. You just stay there on the cold floor.

I saw a boy put in there, and all you could see through the window was him screaming in what Virginia said was a special straitjacket. He was on the floor, screaming in the dark. The jacket didn't look straight to me; it had you tied up in the back so you couldn't get out. After seeing that, I was really scared. I didn't know if saying something wrong or if my mom claiming I did something would get me put in that room. I was terrified. A few days later, Virginia went home and didn't come back. I was all alone in my room and even more scared because my only friend was gone.

Later in the week, one evening, I was in bed sleeping when I heard a noise. I woke up and looked outside my room. There was a light on in the office, and I saw my mom talking to one of the nurses with my little sister Sarah there too. My mom came into my room, brought Sarah, and put her in the bed right next to mine. I pretended to be asleep when she came in, and then she walked out of the room.

She left and then I heard her screaming outside the door saying *"don't take me."* I got scared and woke up, asking the nurse what was going on. The nurse told me to go back to bed and not worry about it. But I couldn't. I was too scared and started crying. My mom's screams of *"Don't take me, don't take me..."* echoed outside. I asked the nurse again what was happening, and she said, "Your mommy is going to stay upstairs in the hospital. Now, go back to bed. "Everything is fine... She just doesn't want to stay that's all but everything is fine don't be scared," she said to me.

I went back to bed and saw my sister sleeping in the empty bed next to mine. Despite everything, I felt a bit happy that Sarah was with me; at least I wasn't alone now. As I lay down, I started to wonder why Sarah was there. My mom never said anything bad about Sarah, so what did she do to end up in the hospital with me?

"Did she think Sarah was evil too, like me?" I thought.

At home, my mom decided Sarah had to stay in the hospital with me. I couldn't sleep well that night, but when morning came, Sarah and I woke up together. We hugged, happy to be reunited. Then the nurses rushed into our room, hurrying us to get in the breakfast line.

Sarah hadn't finished making her bed fast enough, so they started yelling at us. She began to cry. I told her she had to hurry up or they'd yell, something we weren't used to. I tried to help her, but the nurse yelled at me, saying, "No, she has to do it herself." I looked at her and said, "You're mean. That's my sister; I will help her." I helped Sarah, and we made the bed together. Then we went to get breakfast, and Sarah stopped crying.

After breakfast, the nurse told us that since there was no

school, we were going to Central Park. We went to get our sweaters and a toy to bring with us. They asked what kind of toy we wanted: a frisbee, a ball, jacks, or a jump rope. We chose a frisbee and jacks, and I wanted to bring chalk to play hopscotch.

We left for Central Park that day. They brought lunch to the park, so we had lunch there, along with watermelon. There were swings and slides, and Sarah and I had so much fun that it almost felt like we weren't in the hospital. We forgot we were there.

Then they told us we had to go back, so Sarah and I held hands and returned. It was time for dinner, and we washed our hands since they were dirty. We all had to line up to take turns in the bathroom to wash up before heading to the cafeteria for dinner.

There was this big boy in high school who came from a very rich family. All he talked about was the music group ABBA. He loved ABBA, and that's all he wanted to hear. Sometimes, the nurses would put his records on, and we would listen to them. After a while, I got tired of listening to that music.

He would talk about his mom and dad going on Princess Cruises, like on the TV show *The Love Boat*. He said it was the same ship as on the show. I thought he was lying, but the nurse said no, his mom and dad really did go on the Princess Cruises ship, and so did he, but he was sick this time, so they had to leave him behind. I didn't know regular people could go on the Princess Cruise Ship; I thought it was only for people on TV and that the show was made up.

On rainy days when we couldn't go to the park, we stayed inside and learned to play games like Candyland and checkers. Sarah and I had never played Candyland before, so it was new to us. We also spent time in the arts and crafts room, where we discovered painting. I had never painted before, and mixing colors like yellow and red to make orange was a new experience for me. It was a lot of fun, especially with the glitter that made our pictures sparkle.

By October, with Halloween approaching, I still didn't have any shoes. The hospital provided me with paper slippers, but they tore easily as I walked around. Aunt Maria visited and brought me socks while she saved up for a pair of shoes. Meanwhile, Sarah got to go on a pumpkin-picking trip, but I couldn't join her because I didn't have proper shoes.

As Halloween approached, the nurses asked us what we wanted to dress up as. I chose to be Glinda the Good Witch from The Wizard of Oz, and Sarah wanted to be a princess. I asked how are we going to have costumes. The nurse explained that we would make our own costumes. I crafted a wand and a crown for Glinda, using glitter to make them sparkle. Sarah's costume was a poofy princess skirt made from paper.

On Halloween evening, we put on our costumes and went upstairs to the adult psych ward to see my mom. She had made candied caramel apples and handed them to us, beaming with pride. She proudly announced to everyone, "Those are my girls," and told me how pretty I looked. I remember crying, overwhelmed by the realization that she thought I was beautiful.

Afterward, we returned to our floor for a Halloween party. While bobbing for apples, I started to feel unwell, possibly from eating too much candy or from the emotional impact of seeing my mom. That night, I got sick and vomited. I noticed my mom's belly was so big that it seemed the baby would arrive soon, and I assumed she'd have the baby in the hospital.

The following day, the hospital allowed my mom to visit us. She came into the arts and crafts room, sat between Sarah and me, and began to paint. Then she started talking to me and asked me, "Wy are you peeing on top of your sister's head when she is sleeping?

I was shocked... I told her I was not peeing on Sarah's head when she was sleeping.

"I know you are doing that because that is what devil worshipers do," she said.

"Please don't do that, Mom... I'm not a devil worshiper. I don't do that. I say my prayers before I go to sleep as Nagymama taught us to do," I was now crying.

"I know you are peeing on your sister's head," she kept saying. I got up and tried to leave the room, but she grabbed me by the arms, shaking me and screaming. I cried out, begging her to let me go. Two big men intervened, pulling my mom away from me. She continued to chase after me, and two more men restrained her and took her off our floor, and back upstairs.

Then she called downstairs and asked for me. The nurse handed me the phone, but as soon as I picked it up, my mom started yelling at me again. I began to cry, and the nurse noticed. When she asked why I was upset, I explained that my mom was accusing me of being a devil worshiper and peeing on Sarah's head. The nurse quickly took the phone from me and hung it up. She informed me that, from now on, I wouldn't be allowed to speak with my mom until she learned to speak to me respectfully.

A couple of weeks later, the nurse came to Sarah and me with exciting news: Mom had given birth to a baby boy. We were thrilled and immediately asked if we could go upstairs to see him. But the nurse told us that no children were allowed in the nursery—only adults could go there. I asked why and told them that we were his sisters, but the nurse told us we were not allowed to do so.

Even though I was disappointed, I was overjoyed at the thought of having a new baby brother. At eight years old, I felt proud to be his big sister and looked forward to taking care of him when I finally got the chance to meet him. He was my baby brother Mathew.

5

———

A few weeks later, it was almost time for Thanksgiving and we wanted to spend Thanksgiving with Nagymama, Auntie Maria, and our cousins. However, we needed our mom's permission to leave the hospital, and she refused to grant it. She was worried that if she let us go with Aunt Maria and Uncle Luis, they might not bring us back. Despite our pleas, she remained firm. Aunt Maria assured us not to worry, promising she would continue to persuade mom.

Thanksgiving Day arrived, and Aunt Maria and Uncle Luis came to pick us up from the hospital. We spent the day at their house, surrounded by family. I was overjoyed to be with Nagymama, Aunt Maria, Uncle Luis, my cousins, and finally, to meet my baby brother, Matthew.

When Nagymama asked if I wanted to hold Matthew, I eagerly said yes. For the first time, I cradled my baby brother and gave him a big kiss. It was a moment of pure happiness to be with my family. However, in the back of my mind, I couldn't shake the worry about returning to the hospital.

I asked my Aunt Maria what time we had to go back to the hospital. She looked at me, smiled, and said, "Oh... Your uncle and I are not taking you back to the hospital. Your mother was right, we were never planning on taking you back. We lied and told her we were going to take you back but we're not taking you back to the hospital. The only person that needs to be in the hospital is your mother. She's the one that's sick not you and your sister Sarah. You guys don't need to be there... She needs to be there and she's not going to be the boss of you anymore because your uncle Luis and I are going to court so we can be the boss of you and Sarah. This way, she doesn't get to say that she is the boss of you anymore. What do you think about that, Maria?"

I looked at her and I was so happy. I said 'really...' She said, "Yes, sweetheart... Really." I was so happy I went I gave her such a big hug and a kiss and then I ran off and I went to play with my cousins.

So, that Thanksgiving, I got a new baby brother. I got to go live with my Aunt Maria and I had my favorite Hungarian stuffed cabbage with Thanksgiving turkey for dinner and to live with my Nagymama at the same time... I was very happy, that was the best Thanksgiving ever.

After Christmas, Uncle Luis and Aunt Maria spoke with my mom about baptizing Matthew. They decided to plan a big party to celebrate, as in Hungarian culture, having a boy is a significant event, especially in our family.

My mom took on the task of preparing the souvenirs, while Aunt Maria and Uncle Luis transformed the basement of their house into a festive space. Uncle Luis's brother, Papo, was set to be the DJ, and my grandmother, along with Uncle Luis's sisters, handled the cooking. It was going to be a grand celebration, reflecting how much joy Matthew's arrival brought to our family.

The day of the baptism arrived, and the house was packed with over fifty people who had come to celebrate after church. The atmosphere was lively, with everyone dancing. I still remember the songs that played: Dan Hartman's "Instant Replay" and Musique's "In the Bush," both from 1978. Aunt

Maria, however, was the star of the evening when she danced to "Hot Shot" by Karen Young, also from 1978. Her moves were captivating—she wiggled her hips and swayed all the way down to the floor, then back up again. She was an incredible dancer.

That spring, Aunt Maria and Uncle Luis took all of us kids to court, dressed in our best party clothes, the same ones we wore for church. Aunt Maria explained that I would need to speak to an important person about why I wanted to live with her, Uncle Luis, and Nagymama, and why I didn't want to stay with my mom. I went into a room and spoke with a lady and a distinguished man in a robe—he was called The Judge.

I told him that Aunt Maria is very nice to me and Nagymama always takes care of me. I explained that my mommy is sick and crazy in the head, and all she wants to do is beat me up. She thinks I'm a devil worshiper. She's crazy. So, I can't live with her because she might kill me one day. The judge just looked at me and asked:

"Are you scared of your mommy??"

"Yeah, she's crazy... She beat me once with a wooden spoon dipped in boiling water with lots of spices. Another time, she tried to burn me with a cigarette when I was on the chair, but I jumped out of the chair just in time. Whenever my Nagymama isn't looking, she tries to hit me. So yeah, I'm scared of her."

The judge said, "Okay, I think we can make an arrangement for you to live with your Aunt Maria." After that day, we went home, and I knew I didn't have to go back to live with my mom anymore. I lived with my Aunt Maria, Uncle Luis, and Nagymama. I went to school with my cousins in the Bronx, and we all lived in their house. I felt safer there than I ever did with my mom.

My mom came over to visit, and she had a new boyfriend who was Dominican. He gave her money to help with the materials Aunt Maria needed to make me a dress for my First Holy Communion. My cousin Lily and I were both going to have our First Holy Communion and Aunt Maria decided to make our dresses instead of buying them. My mom's boyfriend provided money so Aunt Maria could buy the materials to make the dresses.

That night, my mom and her boyfriend stayed in the living room on the sofa bed with baby Matthew sleeping between them. Matthew cried a lot but finally fell asleep. The next day, I saw her boyfriend slapping her outside while yelling in Spanish. I started crying and asked Aunt Maria and Uncle Luis why he was hitting her. Uncle Luis explained that he was angry because my mom didn't know how to properly take care of the baby, and he blamed her for keeping everyone up all night with Matthew's crying and that she needed to learn how to take care of children better.

I told my mom I didn't need a white communion dress and that I could wear regular clothes for my First Holy Communion. I begged her to leave her boyfriend, telling her I didn't want her to stay with him just for the money to buy me a dress. I told him he was a bad man and that I didn't want him to hit my mom. But she stayed with him, believing it was important for me to have the dress and flowers for the communion.

The day of our First Holy Communion arrived, and Lily and I were excited. Even my Nagypapa showed up at the church. After the ceremony, all our cousins came over to the house, and we had a big party. Nagymama was so proud, she cried that we did our First Holy Communion. It was a big celebration for us.

My uncles Chris and Emmeral came over. Aunt Paula also came with her children and so did my aunt Judith. Aunt Judy was also in attendance with her kids. We had so many people at the house for this party... It was amazing. Even my Uncle Luis's sisters and brothers from upstate New York came down for this party.

Uncle Chris danced with Lily and me, just like John Travolta in *Saturday Night Fever*. Everyone clapped, and we danced to songs from the Village People, the Jackson 5, Donna Summer, Karen Young, and Blondie. Steve, the guy renting a room at my aunt's house, had all of Blondie's music, which I started to like.

After the party, my mom told her boyfriend she was staying with Nagymama and that they were breaking up because he tried to hit her again. He didn't like the way she was dancing. Aunt Maria and Uncle Luis told him he was being ridiculous and made him leave. He refused to go, so they called the police, who made him leave. The next day, Aunt Maria had to go with my mom to the police station to file a report to keep him away.

My mom was scared to go home afterward. Aunt Maria and Uncle Luis suggested she get an order of protection, but Uncle Luis warned her that it might not help much.

"By the time you call the police, he's going to mop the floor with you, and they'll show up after it's too late. So, don't even bother," he said.

Nagymama told my mom she should date a nice Hungarian man instead of all the Spanish men. "This is why you and your sister keep getting beat up," she said.

My mom retorted, "Oh, you mean like the way our dad beat you?"

I turned around and asked Mama, "My papa used to beat you up too Mama...?"

She said, "Yeah, but it was just him... The other man in the family never hit anybody. He was the only bad apple in the bunch."

I said to my Nagymama, "I'm going to marry Elvis Presley or John Travolta when I grow up. I'm not marrying regular men because they hit you and are terrible husbands."

My cousin Lily chimed in, "No, you can't marry Elvis Presley. I'm going to marry him."

Aunt Maria and Nagymama laughed. I asked why they were laughing, and they said he was already married. I said, "Well, he can get a divorce and marry me. I'm prettier than his wife."

Nagymama agreed, "Yes, you are prettier."

I said, "See, when I grow up, he can marry me."

6

One day after school, Aunt Maria and Uncle Luis came home with a man. They called Sarah and me over, saying, "We want you to meet someone."

I asked, "Okay, who is it?"

They introduced him, "This is Carlos. He's a nice man. Go say hello."

Carlos smiled and asked, "Do you like school?"

I replied, "Yeah." Then I added, "So why do I have to meet you?"

"I'm your father."

"I don't have a daddy," I said.

He said everybody has a daddy.

I said, "You're the man who used to beat up my mommy."

"Who told you that?"

"They said that you hit my mommy, that's why you guys got a divorce."

He said, "That's not nice."

"But it's true..."

"Probably..." He goes, "Maria, sometimes grownups do things they shouldn't do. I'm sorry about that."

"Go, give him a hug and a kiss," Aunt Maria told me.

"I don't know who you are even if you are my father."

"Darling, can I have a hug?"

"No! I don't know you, you're a stranger to me."

"But can I have a hug?"

So, I kind of gave him a side hug but I didn't get him a kiss. He goes, "Do you like McDonald's?"

Aunt Maria intervened, "She loves McDonald's. She loves Big Macs..."

"Yeah, I like Big Macs," I said.

He said, "How about if I take all you kids out for McDonald's?"

I said, "Okay, we can go for Big Macs. I Like Big Macs."

"Okay... I'll take you guys out to eat McDonald's... Is it okay?" He asked.

"Sure, but I'm not giving you a kiss," I clarified.

"Okay, sweety! You don't have to give me a kiss."

My sister Sarah said, "I'll give you a kiss."

I asked her not to give somebody a kiss because they give you something.

"That's not right. That's buying your affection. That's not good. Don't do that," I told her.

Carlos laughed and said, "Yeah, listen to your big sister... She's right."

I said, "You see... I told you so."

I met his wife, Amanda. They had a little baby boy so now I

have another half-brother. He's the same age as my little brother Matthew. So, I have two brothers now. He looks a lot like Matthew, but his hair is dark brown while Matthew's is blonde. Carlos's wife seemed nice, but she was quiet and didn't talk much. I don't think she speaks English; she speaks Spanish. She didn't say anything to us kids while we were sitting in McDonald's.

With all of us kids, I think we scared her because there were so many of us. She just had one baby, but with all of us, we were seven kids in total. My cousins are four, and my sister, brother, and I are three, so it was a lot. I don't think she was prepared for seven kids that day. Carlos took us back home and asked if we could visit another day. He asked if I wanted to meet the rest of his family, and I said yes. It would be nice to meet them. I looked at Aunt Maria and asked if it would be okay. She said, "Sure."

We made arrangements for the weekend. Carlos would pick us up—me, Sarah, our grandmother, and my baby brother—to meet the rest of his family. When my mom found out, she decided to come with us.

That weekend, we visited Carlos's family, and I saw my grandmother again. I vaguely recognized her from when I saw her in the hospital long ago when my mom was sick from the birds attacking her in her mind. She was the Spanish lady who gave me the party dress.

I remembered her, I just didn't remember what her name was. My dad said this was his mom, Angela. Oh, yes... Her name was Angela, and she was very kind. She had another big box for me and Sarah, wrapped with a fancy bow and perfume tied to it. Inside was another beautiful party dress, just like before, but different this time. It was very pretty!

I met all my cousins on my father's side of the family, and I couldn't believe how many there were. I couldn't remember all their names, but it was fun to have more cousins to play with, just like my cousins at home. They had a lot of cousins who lived in Upstate New York and I have a lot of cousins now too so it was fun.

"I have my cousins to play with now," I thought in my mind.

My father asked what it was like living at my Aunt Maria's house. I told him the truth: Uncle Luis and Aunt Maria fought a lot but always made up, and we ate rice and beans most of the time. Sometimes we didn't have food, which made him angry. He took us home afterward.

The next day, he came to pick us up again and started yelling at Uncle Luis and Aunt Maria. He took me and Sarah, saying if they wanted us back, they'd have to take him to court.

"So, where are we going to live," I asked.

"With me and your step mother Amanda. I will put you in Catholic school," Carlos said.

That summer, we lived with Carlos, Amanda, and Carlos Jr. Amanda showed me and Sarah how to change Carlos Jr.'s diaper, but unlike Matthew's disposable diapers, Carlos Jr.'s were cloth and needed to be washed. God, it was disgusting...

Amanda made me change his diapers, saying I needed to learn in case of an emergency. When I protested, saying I was his sister, not his mother, she told Carlos, who then yelled at me. He sat us down and laid out the rules: "if we didn't follow them, we'd get hit with the belt. If we get into trouble in school we will get hit with the belt. If we don't watch the baby we will get hit with the belt. If we don't do our chores we will get hit with the belt."

During the summer, we'd go to the beach or the Seven Lakes on weekends and we'd take food with us. Amanda told me to season and fry the chicken. She gave me salt and spices, so I did my best. Afterward, I cleaned up the kitchen and put the chicken away.

The next day at the Seven Lakes, around lunchtime, my aunt took a piece of chicken and said it was too salty and couldn't be eaten. She went to my dad and complained. My father came over, ready to hit me, but my aunt stopped him. She asked why a nine-year-old was seasoning and cooking the chicken. My dad said Amanda was too busy with the baby. I told my aunt that wasn't true; Amanda had been asleep with my dad and made Sarah and me change the baby's diapers.

"The least your wife can do is to teach Maria how to season the meat before cooking it," she said to him.

Then he started yelling at me because he said, you could see my private parts through my shorts and tee shirts. My aunt said to him, "Why don't you buy her a bathing suit?"

"It's the end of the summer. I'll buy her one next year," he replied.

7

School was going to start and we went to this Catholic School in Queens. The Nun had asked my dad if he had our baptismal certificates. He said no. The Nun said you can't register the girls if they are not Catholic.

"My girls were baptized in St. Stephens of Hungary Church," Carlos told the Nun.

She called the church and confirmed our baptism. Then she asked if we did any other sacraments. My father said that I had already done my Penance, and First Holy Communion. He told them the name of that church and they confirmed it. My sister was going to have to begin classes to prepare for Penance, and First Holy Communion. The Nun gave us a schedule and told my father he would have to get us the school uniform as soon as possible. We went home afterward and we were excited to start a new school and to make new friends.

My father dropped us off before heading to work. Amanda was planning to make spaghetti with meat sauce and a chocolate cake for dinner. She asked if we wanted to help, and we agreed, knowing that refusing could mean getting hit with the belt. We learned how to make the meat sauce and cook the spaghetti. The cake was easy since it was just a box mix.

"We never made that kind of cake before," I said to her.

"Really, what kind of cake do you make? She asked.

"My Nagymama makes all kinds of cakes but she does it herself without a box. She puts flour, eggs, salt, sugar, baking powder, and other things."

"She must be a good baker," Amanda said.

"She is the best at cooking too. My Nagymama always lets me help her in the kitchen. When it was time to make the Beigli for Christmas, she would let me open up the walnuts with a small butter knife or she would let me bread the chicken cutlets," I said.

"You must have liked that...," said Amanda.

"I miss being with my Nagymama and sleeping with her," I said to her. Sarah said the same.

Amanda took us to her room and opened up a jewelry box and she had these pretty colorful bracelets. Some were turquoise colored, light green, or blue. She asked us if we liked them and we said yes, they were very pretty. So, she gave us each a bracelet.

The first day of school started. Dad walked us from the house so we could learn the way and walk on our own later. Along the way, we noticed a girl in a uniform and asked if she went to the same school. She said yes. I asked her what grade she was in, and she replied, "4th." I told her I was in 4th grade too and wondered if we might be in the same class.

Dad said, "Now you guys are at school. It's time for me to go to work. I will see you girls later tonight maybe, if you're still awake."

As soon as we got inside, a nun directed Sarah to her class line and introduced her to the teacher at the front. Then, the nun guided me to my line, and I noticed that I was in the same line as the girl we had walked with earlier. The classes that formed the straightest, quietest lines were the first to go upstairs to their classrooms.

My class was one of the last to be called upstairs. Once we were in the classroom, the teacher instructed us to stop talking and moving. Some of the boys, who had been noisy and restless in line downstairs, continued their disruptive behavior in the classroom. The teacher raised her voice and, taking a ruler, slammed it against the chalkboard to get our attention. The boys fell silent and looked at her, bewildered. She walked up to them and sternly declared that, because of their behavior, the entire class would forfeit recess that day. The teacher then assigned each student a seat, and we took possession of those desks for the rest of the year.

The class had officially begun and I already knew that I might be in trouble with my dad even if it was not my fault. These stupid boys are going to be the death of me. At lunchtime, we ate our lunches at our desks. Afterward, the teacher assigned us a punishment: we had to write "I must not talk or fool around" one hundred times. The boys faced additional consequences—they wouldn't have a recess for the entire week and would have to stay after school that day.

Sarah and I went home from school that day and we told Amanda about our first day of school. Amanda told Sarah and me that we needed to make sure to not get into trouble in school. Our dad was not going to tolerate any rule-breaking at all, even if it was not our fault. I started to cry and I was just so scared of getting hit with the belt. Amanda said she didn't think that would happen.

"And besides, I don't think those boys are going to fool around again after today. Remember they have no recess every day this week, and they had to stay after school today? What do you think their parents are going to say to them or give them as a punishment? The boys are not going to do that and if they do,

I will explain it to your father."

"Thank you, Amanda. We did our homework, Amanda."

"Okay girls, put your finished homework on the dining room table. Your father is going to check it when he gets home."

Dad came home late at night after Sarah and I had already gone to bed. He works and goes to college at night. Amanda woke me up and told me to go sit at the dining room table and wait for my father. A few minutes later, he came out of the bathroom in his pajamas.

He asked me, "Maria, did you guess at the math problems?" I said 'no.'

"How did you get these answers?" He asked.

I showed him my work on another page. He saw the work and said, "It's still wrong. They are all wrong, you have to redo your math homework."

"Okay dad but I don't know how to change the answer," I told him.

"I'm going to show you just once and you better learn it correctly or you're going to get hit with the belt."

He showed me how to do the first problem and from that I was able to do the next two problems. Then I needed help again and I went to his bedroom door and I knocked. He asked me to come in.

"What is it?" He asked.

"I need help with a problem," I said.

"I showed you already, didn't you learn anything?" He said.

"Yes, but this problem is different and I can't do it."

"No, you just don't know how to do your math. You're stupid like your mother. She wasn't any good at math either, you're just like her," he was now getting furious.

He came out to the dining room table again and showed me how to do the math fractions and I was able to finish the rest of my math homework. I started to walk towards my room.

"Where do you think you're going?" He asked.

"To bed... I finished the math homework."

"No, now you have to redo your essay, it's too messy. You erased it too many times and it looks messy. You need to rewrite it and you need to watch your penmanship, it's very sloppy."

I rewrote the essay and I showed it to my dad.

"What the fuck took you so long?"

"I'm sorry, I tried to make it neat like you said."

"I'm fucking tired, you took too long Maria. I ought to hit you with the belt just for that."

"No dad, I'm sorry. I will try to do better."

The next morning, Sarah and I were in the kitchen making breakfast as quickly as possible so we could eat fast and leave for school. I was using the spatula to take out the butter and put some of it inside the pan so I could fry my eggs. Dad saw that the butter had some crumbs inside the container and began to yell.

"Who did this? I'm going to have to throw this out... Damn it!!!! Don't you know this costs me money?" He threw the butter container at Sarah and she began to cry.

A few days later in the morning, Sarah and I woke up and

dad told us we were not going to school today.

"How come?" I asked.

"Carlos Jr. is sick, and Amanda has to take him to the doctor. She won't be home in time to meet you girls after school. So, I'm taking you to my grandmother's house. Do you remember meeting her with all your cousins? Her name is Valentina, but everyone calls her Mama. She's my mother Angela's mother."

We took the train from Queens to New York City, heading to Harlem. When we got there, we went into the elevator, which reeked of pee. Sarah and I held our noses to avoid the smell. When we arrived at my great-grandma's apartment, my cousin Diego opened the door. He and his mom lived with Mama. We kissed Mama as soon as we entered the apartment. She told dad that she was in the kitchen cooking sancocho.

He said, "Oh, good... I'm sure the girls will like that later for lunch. I will pick them up after work today. I shouldn't be too late. I don't have class tonight."

Mama gave him a blessing in Spanish and a kiss and he left. Mama had told me and Sarah that we could watch TV or take a nap in her room. When she showed Sarah and me her bedroom, it reminded us of Isabella's grandmother's house. Mama's bedroom had a large bedroom dresser with a mirror. On the dresser were almost ten large statues of saints with rosary beads around them and small clear glass bowls that were filled with holy water and camphor. Then there were plates in front of the saints and African Orishas and on top of the plates was money in bills and coins. She also had dried Indian corn and Vejigante masks.

Sarah and I had lunch and Diego arrived from school. I asked him why Mama had so much stuff on top of the dresser. Diego said that Mama was a Santería and she prayed to those saints and she helped people sometimes.

"Really, how does she help people?"

He explained that sometimes people get desperate in wanting certain things or needing things and she helps them.

"Like when a person wants to have a baby, she tells them which prayers to say and for how long. If someone was looking for love, she could read the tarot cards and tell them when or if they were going to find love."

Dad arrived and he heard me asking Diego about the Santería. He told me, "Don't you dare think about any other religion except the prayers that you learn in school and church. The Roman Catholic Church young lady or you'll get it with the belt. You understand?"

"Yes, I understand..." and with that, we left Mama's apartment. Then dad told me that Carlos Jr. had a really bad ear infection and we had to be quiet when we got home. We got to the apartment and the baby was inside the walker and he was crying.

"The baby is probably in pain," he said, "don't touch the baby, leave him to me and Amanda until he gets better. Do you girls understand?"

We both said "Yes." We both went to our room, put the TV on really low, and closed the door. Then Amanda knocks on the bedroom door and Sarah and I just look at her head for a second. Then she opens the door all the way and brings in Carlos Jr. Amanda and my father both tell Sarah and me that they are going out to the supermarket and that we have to watch the baby. My father said it's quieter at home than it is in the supermarket for the baby. So, he said that we better talk very low and keep our TV volume low. I said "Okay." He yelled at me.

"You're talking too loudly! I said quietly."

I whispered, "Okay."

Later that evening, Amanda and dad got home and found Carlos Jr. sleeping. Dad began yelling at me. "Why did you let him sleep?"

"I didn't know he wasn't supposed to sleep," I said.

"Maria, you FUCKED UP! Now he's not going to sleep at night because he slept already."

Sarah and I went to school the next day and the Nun asked me why don't you have your uniforms yet? I told her that I didn't know and she said that we had to have our uniforms by next week or we would not be allowed back in school. When Sarah and I got home from school, we went to tell dad what the Nun said about us having to have our uniforms for school.

Then the phone rang. It was my grandma Angela. She asked how we were doing in school and how the teachers were treating us. I told her about Sarah and I still not having our uniforms for school. She asked why and I told her that Dad said that he didn't have the money but he would have it soon to get our uniforms. Grandma Angela said she wanted to speak with dad so I gave him the telephone. I heard grandma screaming at my dad on the phone in Spanish. I knew that wasn't good. Then he hung up the phone and started yelling at me.

"Don't you ever tell your grandmother that I don't have the money for anything. Do you understand?"

"Yes, I understand." Then he made Sarah and me go into the living room to count pennies, nickels, dimes, and quarters. Our task was to roll up all the change Dad had been saving in a 10-gallon water bottle. Sarah separated the coins and put them into their proper groups, while I counted the coins to match the amounts on the rolled papers. For example, pennies needed fifty cents, so I made sure to put fifty pennies into the roll. I did the same for all the other coins. Dad took the rolls of coins to the bank and exchanged them for bills. He had enough money to buy uniforms for Sarah and me.

Nagymama and mom came to dad's home to visit. Sarah and I were very excited to see them. We both asked for Mathew, where is he, how is he? They said he's fine but he's with someone. They wouldn't say who. I wanted to know where my brother was so I asked Nagymama. She said she would tell me if I didn't cry or tell Sarah.

"Okay, I promise."

She told me that some nice special people called Foster Parents are taking care of him. She said it was like when Saint Joseph was a father to Jesus even though God was his father. Then my father goes to my mom and tells her that I'm a bad girl because I'm fresh. She wanted to know what I did. He said it was because I didn't put on panties yesterday or today.

My mom said to me, "Why are you not wearing panties? We never raised you like that, what's wrong?"

I told her and Nagymama that I didn't have any clean panties to put on. I ran out of panties and I don't know what to do. My mom explained to Carlos so after my mom and Nagymama left Amanda showed me and Sarah how to use the washing machine. Amanda had said to make sure that the hose that throws out the water is put inside the kitchen sink–inside the deep kitchen sink, not the shallow sink. We wash our dishes in the shallow sink.

"Also make sure to slide over the metal cover from the shallow sink over to the deep sink to hold the water hose in place inside the sink," Amanda said.

Dad asked Sarah and me if we wanted to go to my grandmother Angela's apartment, and we said "No." Then they said since we girls were staying home, we should watch Carlos Jr.

We are home alone watching Carlos Jr. He's about five months old, I am nine years old, and Sarah is six years old. I am trying to do the laundry because I have to wash my panties and I'm not going to get into trouble with my dad. Sarah came and told me that Carlos was wet, his clothes were wet. He peed through his clothes.

"Okay, I will change him, bring me his diaper."

I took off his clothes and started changing his diaper. I opened his diaper and he peed in the air on the sofa. Then Sarah came running to me and said, "Maria, hurry up, the hose came out of the sink and it's throwing out water all over the floor."

"Oh my God, watch the baby!"

I ran to the washing machine and tried to turn it off but it wouldn't stop. I pulled it, turned it, then finally pushed it. The machine turned off, but now there was water everywhere and the baby pooped on the sofa. I first cleaned the baby and told Sarah to watch him. Then I kept mopping up the water with the mop and put the water into the sink. Finally, I was done cleaning up.

"Never again are we staying home alone with the baby, this is too much work." I thought.

Dad and Amanda got home.

"Why is the floor wet? He asked.

I told him about the water spilling out of the washing machine. Then Amanda went over to the sofa and said why is the sofa wet? I told her about Carlos Jr. peeing on the sofa when I was changing his diaper. Dad started yelling and screaming again.

"What the fuck, Maria! Can't you do just one thing, right?? Amanda showed you how to use the washing machine, didn't she? You're stupid just like your stupid mother."

He hit me with the belt one time on my leg, but it was with the buckle end and it really hurt.

"I hate this man; he's so mean to me. Why does he hate me so much?" I thought.

Later that night, I waited for my dad, Carlos, to come into the kitchen just after midnight. He always came for a small sandwich, to smoke pot, and to drink a shot of Puerto Rican rum. I would get up and pretend to go to the bathroom, just to see what he was doing. He never said anything to me about being up late or going to the bathroom while he was smoking, getting high, and drinking.

I needed Carlos to go to sleep because it was really late, and I was tired of waiting for him. Finally, the TV light in his room turned off, and I knew he was asleep. I took his keys, slowly got dressed, and unlocked the door. I left the apartment, locking the door behind me with my dad's keys.

I headed towards the train station but began to panic. Where was I going? Who would I stay with? What about Sarah? I couldn't leave her behind with him. I decided I would have to run away with Sarah another day.

It was peaceful outside, with cars passing by and no one on the streets of Queens. I managed to sneak back into the apartment, lock the door, put my pajamas back on, and go to sleep.

8

———

My mom came over for a visit and it was after school one day. She didn't bring Nagymama because she wasn't feeling well but she was happy to see us and happy to find out that I had gotten my first period. I was kind of embarrassed but she said not to be embarrassed. Later, my dad came out of his room and told me to go to the grocery store. He gave me money and I went by myself. Sarah stayed with mom.

When I got back to the apartment, I found dad sitting on top of my mother on the floor, choking her and banging her head back and forth on the hard-tiled floor. I tried to get him off of her.

I was screaming, "Get off of my mommy, I hate you!"

Finally, he got off of my mother and she grabbed her bag and ran out of the apartment. Then he slapped me and said, "Don't you ever tell me you hate me; you understand?"

"Yes..."

He came after me again. Now, I was trying to get to my room but he had me cornered against the wall just before my room. He slapped me on my belly with the belt and then on my legs. He kicked me and kept yelling, "Don't you ever say you hate me, again."

I got up and ran into my room, crying. I couldn't say it but I felt it, I hated Carlos, I really hated him. I wished we never met him. We were fine before we met him and we were living with Aunt Maria. At least no one hit me at Aunt Maria's house and

64

we had Mathew with us.

The next day, Sarah and I woke up and we both took showers and got dressed for school. I told Sarah to take out her books from her school bag and put the books under the bed. Then I told her to take all of her clean panties out of her drawer and put them in her school bag.

"Why? She asked.

"So, Amanda doesn't see your books here in the house because then she will know," I said.

"What will she know?" She asked again.

"That we are running away from home."

"We're running away from home Maria? We're going to get hit with the belt for running away when dad catches us."

I told her to be quiet before Amanda could hear us. Then I grabbed the change that was on the wall unit in the living room so that we would have a way to pay for the train ride. I filled up my backpack with my panties and Kotex pads for my stupid period.

Now, we were on our way back to Brooklyn. Sarah asked me where we were going. I said Brooklyn of course, where else? What train are we going to take? I told her the same train dad took us on to New York City then we would take the shuttle then change to the double LL line to Graham Avenue, and walk upstairs to Isabella's grandma's house. That is exactly what we did and we arrived at Ma's house later that morning and went upstairs. We saw Ma talking to some people and then she said to Sarah and me, "What are you two doing here?"

"We ran away from home and we came here so we can live

with Isabella. We don't want to live with our dad Carlos anymore, he's very mean. He hit me and he beat up my mom."

Ma said "I know; your mother came over here crying and talking about how badly your father had beaten her. She was so scared of him, the poor thing. I felt very sorry for your mother. But there is no need to worry about your mother anymore, she's at home safe with your grandmother. Now, are you girls hungry?"

"Yes, we're starving..."

"Oh, that's good because we have lots of oatmeal and cereal and bacon to eat. Would you like some?"

We said "yes," and with that, we began stuffing our mouths with more food than we could chew, washing it down with chocolate milk. Isabella finally showed up, and though it was the evening, she asked what we were doing there. We began telling her what had happened at our apartment with our dad, our mom, and me.

I told Isabella that I hated Carlos and wished we had never met him. We were fine before he came into our lives. He's a very mean, angry, and scary man. Isabella told us that we couldn't stay with her because she wasn't old enough and wasn't married, things she needed to properly raise two children. We didn't understand, but she said we could spend the night and that she would talk to the police the next day about how violent Carlos was.

The next day, Isabella went to the police station and explained everything. The police contacted my dad, my school, and the nuns at my school. The nuns showed up at the station to meet with Isabella. When my dad, Carlos, arrived, the police,

Isabella, and the nuns confronted him. They told him they knew what he had done to me and my mother and that it would not be allowed to happen again. They warned him he would go to jail if he hit me again.

Carlos saw Sarah and me at the station. A police detective took statements from both of us. Afterward, the nuns spoke to us, telling us to report to them anytime Dad hit us. The police and Isabella then turned us over to Carlos. We got into the car with him, with Sarah and I both sitting in the back seat.

Carlos drove a few blocks, then stopped the car and parked. He turned around and yelled, "Don't either one of you dare speak a word to each other. You are not allowed to talk or look at each other unless I say so. Got that?"

He continued driving, yelling and shouting at us the entire way from Brooklyn to Queens. When we arrived at the apartment, Carlos told Sarah to sit on the sofa in the living room and ordered me to sit on my sister's twin-size bed facing the wall.

"Don't look anywhere else, don't get up, no watching TV, no nothing. You got that!" He closes the door to my bedroom and goes to the living room. I can hear him yelling at Sarah.

"What did she say? Why did you listen to her? From now on, you don't listen to her unless you want to get it with the belt."

Oh my God... He doesn't care if they throw him in jail for hitting us. He really is evil. Then the door to my room opened and he told Sarah to sit where I was sitting. Then he told her the same thing, "face the wall and don't talk, or look anywhere else but straight forward." He made me sit in the living room and began questioning me.

"Why did you go? What did you think was going to happen? If you think I care about being thrown in jail, you're nuts. They put me in jail for a few hours then they sent you home a few hours later. It's not like I am going to jail for years. And when I get out, you're going to get a worse beating."

He took a plastic hanger and hit me on my back a couple of times.

"That's not going to show a bruise on you right away."

Then he sent me to my room.

The next day, I went to school and I told the Nun that my father hit me with the hanger on my back. She took me aside and lifted my shirt to look.

She said to me, "Well yes, you are definitely bruised but he hasn't broken the skin. As long as you're not bleeding or have broken bones. Yes, don't you understand? If there is nothing broken or bleeding then it's not that serious. I have children here that get beaten much worse than that and they don't eat either most of the time at home. Those children most of the time eat here in school, so you are most fortunate."

So, I went to class and later, I went home with Sarah. We had dinner that night and Carlos was home having dinner with us as well. He made us drink milk with our dinner. When we were done with dinner, I started washing the dishes as Sarah started clearing the table.

All I could think of was bleeding and broken bones, that's what she said. The Nun said that if I didn't have either one of those, they wouldn't say or do anything to Carlos. So, he can keep on hitting me however he likes. That entire night, I was thinking of running away again but where and with who? Who can we go to that's not going to give us back? Aunt Maria, but I'm not going to say anything to anyone.

It's Saturday. Sarah and I were awake, but we didn't turn on the TV. If we did, Amanda would bring baby Carlos for us to watch, and we didn't want to watch him. He cried all the time, and every time he did, Dad came into our room and got angry, blaming us for Carlos Jr. crying and saying he couldn't sleep.

Sarah went to the bathroom, and Amanda heard the door. She brought the baby into the room with a clean diaper and a change of clothes. In the back of my mind, I thought this was going to be the last time I watched this kid. He's not my brother because I hate his father, Carlos.

To me, Carlos is just the man my mother married and had me and my sister with. He was never there for us. He never kissed our pain away. He never hugged us or held our hands. He never wiped away our tears or chased away the monsters from our bad dreams. He yells at us, scares us, hits us, and curses us. He has money to buy pot to get high but not enough to buy our school uniforms. He's a terrible father.

I had it all planned out in my mind, what we were going to do. However, I couldn't say anything to Sarah because he threatened her so badly, she's so scared of him, it's like he's the devil. I would only let her know what to do as we were getting to the next steps or stages. The door opened to my room, and it was my dad.

"What's going on in here? I can't sleep with all this noise."

I said sorry, but he told me he was kidding. He was already awake, but if the baby was really making that noise, I would be in trouble.

"So, watch it, young lady," he said. I told him I would. Then Carlos told me to get a pencil and paper, so I did. He instructed me to follow him into the kitchen, where he gave me a breakfast grocery list. It started with his coffee, milk, orange juice, then eggs, bacon, and bread.

"Take your sister Sarah with you because that's too much stuff and you'll drop it. Remember, you two are not allowed shoes on, no socks. You can either wear your sandals or flip-flops and no coats—you can wear your sweaters."

"Carlos, it's too cold for the girls to go to the store without a coat and closed shoes or boots. Look, there's snow outside, and you know Maria has asthma," Amanda said.

"I said no! They can't have coats or shoes. The girls are only allowed closed shoes and a coat when they go to school. It has to be this way so that it's difficult for them to run away," he replied.

Carlos gave us the money for the groceries. As soon as we got out of the building, we headed towards the grocery store. On either side of the block where the grocery store was, there were staircases that led to the train station. I asked Sarah, "Which side of the train station entrance do you like?"

She looked at me and said, "No, we are not going anywhere. Listen, I get hit, you don't. I'm not staying and waiting for Dad to beat me up whenever he feels like it. I know where we can go, and those people will help us no matter what."

"Where?"

"I'm not going to tell you until we're almost there, just in case we get caught. I don't want you to get into as much trouble as me."

Sarah agreed, and we went into the train station, bought tokens, and boarded a train. The train took us to New York City, which was perfect. From there, we took the shuttle, then the number six train to Parkchester Avenue in the Bronx. We had a long walk to my Aunt Maria's house.

Finally, we reached Aunt Maria's house and were so happy to get inside. It was warm, and all my cousins were there, along with my Nagypapa. I had never seen my Nagypapa at Aunt Maria's house. It didn't matter—my Nagypapa was there now. I asked my cousin Lilly where Aunt Maria was. She said her mother was upstairs with the tenants and friends.

My Nagypapa asked, "Why are you running?"

"To find Auntie Maria before my father Carlos finds me and my sister. He's a bad man, Papa. He beat up Mommy once. He hits me and yells at me. I'm afraid of Carlos."

My Nagypapa said Aunt Maria was upstairs and not to worry. He wasn't going to let my father near me. He kissed the top of my head, as he always did, and reminded me that no man or boy should kiss me anywhere other than the top of my head or my hand. My grandfather was very old-fashioned but very proper with the children in the family.

He gestured for me to go upstairs, so I did. "Aunt Maria, Aunt Maria," we called, running up the spiral staircase. We gave her a big hug and kiss. She said, "Thank God your father came to his senses. Where is he?"

"Well, um, he's at home. We kind of ran away from home. He's always yelling and hitting me, and he even beat up Mom. We ran away before to Isabella's house, but they made us go back. We don't want to live with him. He's very mean. Look at my back."

Aunt Maria lifted my shirt to see the bruises and was furious. She said, "Get downstairs right now."

Sarah and I went downstairs, and Aunt Maria showed my back to my Nagypapa. Then she screamed for my Uncle Luis and showed him too. The adults made a decision about where to hide Sarah and me. Aunt Maria, Sarah, and I went to the Port Authority, where Aunt Maria bought us a bus ticket to Upstate New York. My Nagypapa stayed home to watch my cousins, and Uncle Luis had to go to work.

When we arrived, it was Uncle Luis's sister, his brother, and mother, and all the rest of his family who lived there. Aunt Irene answered the door, happy to see us. She gave us all hugs and kisses and asked Aunt Maria where Uncle Luis was and what was going on.

Aunt Maria explained the entire story. She asked, "Can the girls stay with you just for a little while? It's only until your brother and I can go to court and get temporary custody of them."

"Yeah, okay, sure. Just let me know how things are going. Check-in from time to time. Oh, and here, this is a few bucks so you can buy groceries for all the kids. If you need more, just let me know."

"No, Maria, we're good. Don't worry about it."

Aunt Irene turned to us and said, "Right girls, we are going to have fun. Wave goodbye to your Aunt Maria." Then she showed us the kids' room. She took her youngest son out of the bottom bunk and put him to sleep with her. She took her youngest daughter out of the other bunk and put her to sleep with the oldest daughter. "Okay, Sarah and Maria, you each have your own bed. You're only going to be here for a little while, so don't get sad. Your Aunt Maria will fix things. While you're here, you'll have fun with my kids."

"Okay, Aunt Irene, we won't get sad."

9

———

During our time in Upstate New York, we played in the snow, went to the park, and spent time with our cousins. I even helped them with their homework. Sarah and I were happy. I spoke with Aunt Irene and asked if she thought Aunt Maria would come to get us soon, as we had already been there for several weeks. She told us to be patient because it takes time for the judge to decide on custody, especially during the holiday season when the courts are backed up with many cases.

"Will Aunt Maria get custody by Christmas, do you think, Aunt Irene?' I asked.

"I'm not sure, but I am sure she is trying her best and will be here as soon as possible," she replied.

Sarah and I looked at each other, hopeful that by Christmas, we would be living with Aunt Maria, Uncle Luis, and our cousins. On Christmas Eve, we were very sad. Aunt Maria still hadn't picked us up, and we asked everyone if it was her whenever the phone rang. It was never her, and Aunt Irene said not to be upset because Santa Claus was coming that night.

"Santa Claus will bring you toys tonight, but only after you go to sleep,' Aunt Irene said.

I whispered to Aunt Irene, "I know there's no such thing as Santa Claus. I'm not a baby."

She looked at me and said, "That's not true. There really is a Santa Claus."

"I don't care. I want my Aunt Maria and my brother Matthew. I want everything to go back to normal again."

"Why did that stupid man, Carlos, have to come around? I hate him. Carlos ruined my family, and I miss everybody. He even beat up my mom," I told Aunt Irene, unable to stop crying. She hugged me and Sarah.

"Don't worry. No matter what, your Aunt Maria will make sure everything is fixed, and you'll go back to her," Aunt Irene assured us.

"Are you sure?" I asked.

"Yes, I'm sure. She's your mother's sister and has always been there for her. Before you were even born, your mother and your aunt did everything together. They went to school, shopped, and attended school dances together. They even went on double dates with your father and uncle," she explained.

"What's a double date?" I asked.

"That's when one couple goes out on a date and invites another couple to join them, so they're not alone," Aunt Irene said. "Your Aunt Maria always tried to help your mother."

Later that night, we watched *Rudolph the Red-Nosed Reindeer* and were then sent off to bed because "Santa Claus is coming." I knew there was no Santa Claus, but I didn't say anything to Sarah because she was younger and still believed.

In the morning, my cousins woke us up, saying there were presents for us. I thought it was strange because neither my mom nor my Nagymama or Aunt Maria were there. Who could have bought us presents? Sarah got a doll that wets itself after being fed, and she looked at me saying, "Who wants to change more stupid diapers?"

"Not me," I said, and she agreed, "Not me either. I think we've had enough of changing diapers."

Sarah also received a Colorforms wardrobe set, where you could mix and match clothes on a plastic board. I got a train full of lip balms, each with a different scent. They didn't give any color when applied, but they smelled nice. I also received a necklace with matching earrings. They were nice, but I still wanted my other cousins and Aunt Maria.

We had breakfast and watched TV all day. Later that night, we heard people singing "Feliz Navidad!" at the door. Aunt Irene told Sarah and me to open the door together. We did, and the singing got louder. It sounded terrible, but it was funny. When we opened the door, it was Aunt Maria and Uncle Luis. I started to cry with happiness, hugging and kissing them. They apologized for coming late, explaining they had just received the custody papers the previous day and had car trouble that day.

Sarah and I were so happy, jumping up and down. We showed Aunt Maria our Christmas presents and told her how nice Aunt Irene had been to us. Uncle Luis asked if they could spend the night, and Aunt Irene agreed, although everyone would be spread out between the three apartments. Some would stay in Aunt Irene's apartment, others in Uncle Papo's, and the rest in Uncle Luis's mother's apartment.

That night, everyone got split up, and we all slept wherever there was room. My cousin Lilly slept with Sarah and me, and we talked about going home together the next day and attending the same school again. It was going to be great, especially when Aunt Maria got my brother Matthew back from foster care. We could all live together again, just like before Carlos showed up.

The next morning, Aunt Irene said she wanted to come stay

with us for a few days. Aunt Maria said that would be wonderful. Uncle Luis was outside working on the car and called for me.

"Maria, come outside," he said.

Aunt Maria asked, "What for?"

He replied, "Not you, little Maria. You heard your uncle, go outside."

I went outside and called my uncle, who was underneath the car. He came out and said, "You're going to push the gas pedal when I say 'go ahead' and stop when I say 'stop.' Understand?"

"Yes, I understand," I said.

He looked at the motor from the front of the car and held the hood open with a stick. "Push," he instructed, and I pushed. "Stop," and I stopped. "Aha, that's it, you bastard. Push again." I pushed. "Stop." I stopped.

"Okay, Maria, you can go back inside and play, but just for a little while. Tell both of your aunts that we're going to be leaving very soon, and for them to be ready. I hate to wait."

"Okay, Uncle Luis, I will tell them."

I informed both of my aunts, and Aunt Maria said that Uncle Luis has no patience for waiting on people. She yelled for everyone to get dressed because we were leaving soon. We all grabbed our toys and bags of clothes and put them in the car. A few minutes later, all nine of us kids piled into the car, along with Uncle Luis, Aunt Maria, and Aunt Irene—twelve of us in a 1978 Oldsmobile Cutlass. We were sitting on each other's laps because there was no room, and none of us used seat belts for the two-hour drive from Upstate New York to the Bronx.

Finally, we arrived in the Bronx, back with Aunt Maria and Uncle Luis. Now we just had to get my baby brother Matthew back.

Aunt Irene asked my cousin Elizabeth and my sister Sarah to go to the store and buy her a pack of cigarettes. Aunt Maria added that they should also pick up a pack for her and a six-pack of beer for Uncle Luis.

"Okay, Mom, I will get it," Elizabeth replied.

Aunt Maria looked outside to see what was taking the girls so long and saw Sarah yelling, "Don't grab me! Don't grab me!" She rushed outside and saw Carlos trying to grab Sarah. Aunt Maria yelled for Uncle Luis, and Aunt Irene screamed for him too, telling someone to call the cops. The police arrived, and I got scared, hiding under the table.

Aunt Maria came inside for the custody papers and handed them to the officers, explaining that she had legal custody of us. Carlos, visibly upset, had to leave without Sarah. Aunt Maria told me it was safe to come out from under the table.

"Don't worry. He's not going to bother you anymore," she assured me.

I felt relieved knowing Carlos couldn't take us away anymore.

10

───────

A week later, Aunt Maria came home with my brother Matthew, who had all these new clothes packed in his suitcase. He was big now, walking by himself like a big boy, not a tiny baby anymore. We were so happy to see him. As it was almost nighttime, we knew we had to get ready for bed, so I asked Aunt Maria if we could give him a bath. She said yes. My cousin Lily and I bathed him, and found pajamas, a robe, and slippers in his suitcase. We thought how fancy! We had never had a robe or slippers for him before.

Uncle Luis saw him in his new clothes and said he looked better off over there than here, as we couldn't afford any of this stuff. Lily and I laughed and thought, "Don't be silly, Uncle Luis. He's better off with us, with family."

Aunt Maria had all of us kids sleeping in the large bedroom, which had one queen-sized bed and two bunk beds. The bedroom next to us had my aunt and uncle's friend, Steve, living there, and my aunt and uncle had the front bedroom. We really liked Steve. He was a lot of fun and had all the latest records and videos for music that played on the radio.

It was 1980, and Queen had just come out with "Another One Bites The Dust." The Sugarhill Gang released "Rapper's Delight," Ray, Goodman & Brown had "Special Lady," The Whispers had "The Beat Goes On," Jermaine Jackson had "Let's Get Serious," and the SOS Band had "Take Your Time." These were all hit songs we listened to on the radio and constantly at home. We danced to them, and Steve played them over and over again for us, making us very happy on the weekends.

My mom and Nagymama came over for the weekend to visit, and Steve just stopped and looked at my mother like a ton of bricks hit him over the head. I don't know what came over him, but he introduced himself to my mom. She said hello, and he walked out the door, saying he was going out with some friends. My mom and Nagymama brought over chocolate brownies that my grandmother had made for all of us kids. Aunt Maria asked my mom what she thought about Steve. My mom said he was kind of bald but okay. Aunt Maria said, "Yeah, he's a nice guy. You really should look into going out with him."

"What the hell are you talking about? Why would I want to go out with him?" my mom asked.

"Because he's a nice guy, and you should see how good he is with the kids. He's great with the kids. They love him, and he's a lot of fun," Aunt Maria replied.

My grandmother and Aunt Maria finished making Hungarian stuffed cabbage, and Steve showed up back at the house. My mom said, "Hi Steve, I see you're back."

"Oh yeah, hi. It's nice to see you again," Steve replied.

Aunt Maria asked him, "Steve, would you like to have some stuffed cabbage? Hungarian stuffed cabbage?"

He said he had never had it before. She told him to sit down, and she'd serve him a plate. "You're going to like this," she said.

"I don't know if I'll like it," he replied.

She said, "Taste it. I'll give you a little bit, and you try it."

So, he tried it, tasted it, and really liked it. Steve told Aunt Maria that he really loved the stuffed cabbage and asked her to thank my grandmother for cooking it.

I asked Steve if I could borrow the "Rapper's Delight" record by The Sugarhill Gang for a class party at school. Steve said sure, as long as I promised to bring it back and not lose it. I assured him I wouldn't lose it and would take care of it.

Steve then asked my mom out for a date to dinner and a movie. They went out, and afterward, my mom asked me if I liked Steve. I told her, "Yeah, he's fun, and I like the videos and records he has."

A few months later, my mom and Steve got engaged to be married.

My Aunt Maria told me that I would be going to my mom's for Thanksgiving this year with Steve, my sister, and my brother. We'd be staying over at the apartment with my grandmother for the entire weekend. However, on Sunday, I had to tell Steve not to bring us back home because Aunt Maria was leaving Uncle Luis, so nobody would be there. Steve wasn't to bring us back on Sunday because we wouldn't be going to school on Monday.

We went to my mother's house in Brooklyn for Thanksgiving dinner. I waited until Sunday, as Aunt Maria instructed, and then told them before it was time to leave that we couldn't go back to Aunt Maria's because she wouldn't be there. My mom said we still had to go because Aunt Maria has sole custody. Steve insisted he would take us back, no matter what, and that we could stay with Uncle Luis until things were sorted out.

When we arrived at Aunt Maria's house, there was no heat, no toilet paper in the bathroom, and no food in the refrigerator—no milk, no bread. The cupboards were bare, and it was colder inside the house than outside. My sister Sarah and I looked at Steve, saying, "What are we supposed to do? It's freezing here!" Steve replied he didn't know, but maybe Uncle Luis would have answers. I pointed out that Uncle Luis wasn't there. We only had two diapers with us, which was enough for tonight and tomorrow morning. Matthew needed more than that. Steve asked if there were more diapers in the house, and I said someone must have taken them all.

Steve told Sarah and me to go to sleep, and he would take us back to my mother's apartment in Brooklyn in the morning. We would figure things out during the week. I didn't sleep at all that night because it was so cold. I gathered as many blankets as possible and covered my younger sister and brother so they could sleep. Eventually, they fell asleep, but I couldn't. The cold air made me cough and wheeze due to my asthma. Despite my discomfort, I was relieved they were asleep, so I watched over them through the night.

In the morning, Steve told us we had to hurry and get dressed. He took us to my mom's apartment in Brooklyn, where we finally had breakfast and it was warmer. I managed to take a nap and slept the entire day, only waking up when it was dark outside. I couldn't believe I had slept through the day. Steve called the house, saying that Aunt Maria had not returned, and he had spoken to Uncle Luis. We would stay with my mom and Nagymama until Aunt Maria came back or until Steve heard from her.

A few days later, Steve called again, saying Aunt Maria had returned and he would pick us up to take us back to the Bronx. My mom said we could now return to living with Aunt Maria in the Bronx.

Lately, Aunt Maria has been very sad. She cries often and has Steve drive her to a special diet doctor. She's taking pills and trying to lose weight to be skinny for Uncle Luis, who she says is seeing someone else because she isn't skinny enough. She wants to become very thin like Sandy in the movie *Grease*. My cousin Lily and I thought Aunt Maria was crazy, but Aunt Maria always believed she was fat and thought Sandy was beautiful because she was very skinny. She said all women should be skinny. Aunt Maria told Lily and me that when we grow up, we needed to be very thin because men only liked skinny women.

Aunt Maria also stopped going to work and began staying in bed, crying and being moody. I overheard her on the phone with my mother, saying, "If you don't send over your food stamps so I can put a chicken on the table for your kids, then they're not going to eat. I don't have any food to put on the table for your kids. Do you think it's easy to feed three kids and my four? That's seven kids! What do you think I'm made of, money? I didn't stop working because I wanted to. I lost my job, and that's why I'm home."

One gray, cloudy morning, as we kids put on our backpacks and prepared to head out the door, Uncle Luis said to my sister Sarah and me, "You girls might want to start running away again."

Aunt Maria quickly interrupted, "Stop that! Don't say things like that to them."

Sarah and I exchanged confused glances—why would he say something like that?

When we got home from school, Aunt Maria told me, "Maria, pack your clothes into a black garbage bag. Do the same for Sarah and Matthew. Give your school books to your cousin Lily; she can take them back to school for you and Sarah."

I nodded and asked, "Okay, Aunt Maria. What else?"

"That's it. Just be ready. Someone will come to pick you up."

I asked, "Who's coming to pick us up, and where are we going?" She replied, "Don't worry about who's picking you up or where you're going. Just do as you're told."

I turned to Aunt Maria and noticed Baby Matthew had peed through his clothes. I asked, "Why doesn't he have a diaper on?" She yelled at me and smacked Baby Matthew, saying, "Stop peeing through your clothes." I protested, "But he's still a baby." Aunt Maria replied, "He needs to learn. Where you're going, they probably won't put a diaper on him anymore. He's a big boy now and he's walking." I said, "That's crazy. He's still a baby and doesn't know any better."

Just then, the doorbell rang. A tall African-American man with a heavy accent I couldn't understand entered. He asked, "Are you ready?"

I looked at him, unsure why I should go with a stranger. He said, "You have to come with me. I'm taking your little sister and brother."

I insisted, "Don't touch them—I'll take them."

He said, "That's fine, but you still have to come with me."

I turned to Aunt Maria and said, "You're giving us away to this man."

She responded, "I'm not giving you away. You're going to live with a nice family that will take good care of you."

I replied, "Oh, how nice. You're giving us away."

We got into the backseat of the car. I asked the man if he could buy diapers for Matthew. He said, "Yes, after I pick up this lady, I'll get you diapers."

We drove from the Bronx into New York City. The drive seemed endless, and I kept reminding the man to get diapers for Matthew. Aunt Maria said she couldn't afford any, so Matthew peed through his clothes and was hit for it. I insisted on getting diapers quickly.

The man agreed, and when the lady entered the car, he instructed her to buy diapers. She asked what size Matthew used, and I told her size 4. We stopped at a convenience store where she bought a box of diapers.

With Matthew now in a diaper, I felt relieved. It was late at night, and we had been driving for over two hours through dark, empty countryside. I wondered where we were being taken.

When we arrived at a house, it was too dark to see well. The man unloaded our things and led us to the front door. A woman greeted us and invited us in. Inside, there was her husband and several older kids, all staring at us. The man disappeared as soon as we entered, leaving me anxious. I held Sarah close and carried Matthew in my arms, warning the older kids to stay away or I'd have to bite them. A teenage boy laughed and said, "Oh boy, check her out. She's spunky."

The man, who introduced himself as Derrick, and the woman, named Karen, were very kind. Karen reassured us, "You don't have to be scared. No one will hurt you here. I promise."

The teenage boy, named Donald, kept teasing me. Karen told him, "Donald, cut it out or I'll let her bite you to death."

I stuck out my tongue and liked Derrick, who helped us settle into our new rooms.

We were placed in the downstairs basement. Sarah and I had two twin beds with a nightstand between us and a bureau without a mirror. There was a walk-in closet for extra clothes. Matthew had a twin bed across from our dresser. I asked about another twin bed in the room, and they said it belonged to a boy named Mike, who was at a friend's house but would be home soon. Karen asked if Matthew would sleep in his own bed, and I agreed, unless Mike caused trouble, in which case I'd have to bite him to death.

A little while later, Mike showed up and we all met him. He seemed to be very nice and friendly.

11

———

The next morning, Sarah and I woke up to see the older boys outside shoveling snow. Matthew came upstairs, and Donald, playing too rough, threw him to the ground. Matthew kept saying, "Stop," but Donald didn't listen. Finally, Karen heard Matthew's screams and told Donald to stop.

Later, Karen took Sarah, Matthew, and me to the salon for haircuts, then to the doctor, and finally to the school we would be attending. She informed us, "You girls will start school on Monday." We agreed and spent the rest of the day grocery-shopping with her. She had the shopping routine down to a science, stopping at the bread store, grocery store, meat market, and discount store. Karen even bought birthday and special occasion cards in advance to avoid paying full price.

Back home, we helped unpack the car. Sarah and I asked the other girls, Jenny and Peggy, where everything went. They showed us the spots for all the items, and once we finished, we helped make dinner. We prepared tuna salad, macaroni and cheese, soup, and a tossed salad.

At dinner, Donald rushed everyone because he had soccer practice at the high school. His mom, Karen, told him to calm down. As I reached for the tuna salad, Donald called me a "lard ass." I responded, "I am not, and you should take that back."

He stubbornly replied, "No, you're definitely a lard ass."

Upset, I ran into the bathroom. Karen and Donald's older brother, John, knocked on the door, asking me to come out. I liked John better; he was kind and didn't bother anyone. Karen insisted that Donald apologize, but he refused. I told Karen it was fine because I didn't want a fake apology anyway.

Monday arrived, marking our first day at the new school in the suburbs. Sarah was taken to her class first, then it was my turn. The classroom was clean, neat, and quiet, complete with its own bathroom. The school was free of graffiti, and so far, I only saw white students. After the Star-Spangled Banner was played over the loudspeaker, they announced the birthdays for the day. I thought that was very nice—something we never had at our schools in Brooklyn or the Bronx.

Lunch was delicious, and I enjoyed it immensely. The gym class followed, and it was quite challenging. A boy in our class, who did gymnastics, demonstrated how to use the horse and the parallel bars. I wanted to learn gymnastics, but it seemed difficult.

When Sarah and I got home from school, Matthew was crying. We asked him why, and he said Jenny and Peggy wouldn't let him watch cartoons. I asked the girls why he couldn't watch TV, and they said it was because they were watching soap operas—All My Children and General Hospital. I tried explaining that Matthew was a baby and needed to watch TV, but they didn't care. Donald was wrestling with Matthew again, and he was screaming. I asked Karen to intervene, but she didn't. Derrick came home, and I told him about Donald being a bully. Derrick sent Donald to his room, but that seemed insignificant since Donald spent most of his time there anyway.

The first month passed, and Karen gave Sarah and me money. We asked what it was for, and she explained that it was for our chores and our clothing allowance from the foster care agency. We received this allowance monthly, except in October, November, and December, which was explained as a way to save up for Christmas presents.

As spring arrived, adjusting to this new family remained difficult. They frequently called each other names and picked on us for no reason. Karen didn't care and would yell at us if we defended ourselves. She was also putting us on a diet.

Our first Easter with the Johnsons started with excitement as we discovered beautiful Easter baskets upstairs. However, things quickly soured when Peggy hit me on the head with an egg. I jumped up, shocked, and asked why she did that. She then bashed me on the back of the head with another egg. Angered, I searched for a pot to retaliate. I couldn't understand the point of this tradition. Jenny explained that it was a game where you hit each other with eggs to find the hidden ones. I thought it was absurd.

I went downstairs and told Peggy that if she didn't stop, I'd slap her. We then went to Karen's brother's apartment in Queens for Easter dinner. Being reminded of our family in New York City, I couldn't help but feel abandoned. We spent the holidays with strangers who were paid to care for us, and their children bullied us. We had to pretend to be happy, even though we felt alone and unwanted.

I wonder what happened to Anna and her daughter Agota, the ballerina from Queens. The only person I'm not missing is Carlos, and there's nothing that would make me regret his absence.

It's Sarah's birthday, and my mom and Steve came over with my grandmother, who met Karen and her husband, Derrick. My mom announced that she and Steve were married now and asked Sarah and me if we were impressed by the big house, the spacious backyard, and the swimming pool. She also asked if we planned to stay here forever and if we wanted to be adopted. I told her we don't want to be adopted by these people.

"They are very different from us—they aren't Hungarian and don't understand us. Their son, Donald, keeps calling me a "spick." He says it's because I'm Puerto Rican, but I don't see why that matters since I'm only 10 years old," I told her.

My mom confronted Karen about Donald's behavior. "What's going on in your house? Why do you let your son speak to my daughter like that?"

Karen responded, "No, of course not, Lily, but you know how kids are. My kids would never say anything like that." My mom pointed out that this family didn't go to church, unlike when we used to attend every day before school. She also noted that the family seemed to hate each other and that Karen allowed it.

Karen insisted that she didn't permit anyone to pick on each other or harbor hatred. But when I told Karen that Donald was bothering Matthew and not listening to me, Karen brushed it off.

"He doesn't listen to anybody because you're just talking. You don't discipline him; you let him get away with everything. He has no chores or responsibilities, and he's always disrespectful," I said.

Karen retorted, "Maria, it sounds like you just have a problem with Donald. You're making it seem like he's the issue because he's my son and makes me look bad."

My mom told Karen that Donald's behavior makes her look

prejudiced and incapable of managing him. Karen dismissed this, claiming Donald was just "high-spirited" and that I was exaggerating.

A month later, it was my birthday, and my mom returned for the celebration. Marcia, a friend of Karen's who had a dozen kids, also joined the party. After my mom left, Karen and Marcia came downstairs to find Donald rubbing against Sarah and jumping on the bed with her.

Marcia said, "You shouldn't let Donald play like that with Sarah. She's only eight, and he's seventeen. It doesn't look right, no matter how innocent it seems. I don't allow my boys to behave like that with my girls, even though they're all related."

Karen reacted by yelling at Donald to stop and not to do it again. It's ironic how she was suddenly reacting to Donald's behavior when I raised the same issue weeks ago and was told I was being too sensitive. According to Karen, nothing ever goes wrong in her house.

My mom started getting weekend visitation rights, which meant that the three of us could stay with her on weekends. If these visits went well, she might regain full custody. This time, she seemed to be managing better. She was taking her medication, seeing her doctors regularly, and was genuinely kind to us.

Steve and Mom picked us up on Friday night and drove us back to our old apartment in Brooklyn. Sarah and I were excited to see Bell and Maritza again—it had been a long time. We also saw David Jr., his sister Lizette, and Bell's daughters, Jane, Angie, and Susie. It felt good to be back in Brooklyn.

Nagymama was at the apartment waiting for us, and as

always, she had been cooking. I had missed her cooking so much. We hated the meals at the Johnsons' house—always pasta from a box with jarred tomato sauce. The food was bland, with overcooked vegetables and bitter sauce. Hungarian food, on the other hand, was always made from scratch and full of flavor. We had stuffed cabbage, breaded pork chops with pasta and potatoes in paprika sauce, and creamed sweet peas. Our meals were anything but dull. I especially loved our desserts—Nagymama's Hungarian crepes, chestnut puree with whipped cream, and my favorite, Dobos Torte. This cake had seven layers of chocolate and a hard caramel top layer; it was the best dessert ever.

When I asked Nagymama what she made for dinner, she said it was stacked potatoes with stuffed chicken and brownies. It sounded wonderful. I asked her when we could eat, and she said we could eat now.

Mom told Sarah and me to take a shower. I asked if we should go one at a time, but she said we had to shower together. "Why?" I asked. "Just do it," Mom insisted. Sarah and I went into the bathroom. I adjusted the water, but Sarah complained it was too hot, so I made it cooler. Mom came in and said she'd adjust the water herself but first wanted to check our bodies.

"Check our bodies for what?" I asked, my mind racing.

"Anything! I don't know what you've been up to these past few months."

Mom examined Sarah and asked about a red mark on the back of her knee. Sarah didn't know how it got there. Mom questioned her repeatedly, but Sarah insisted I hadn't hurt her. Afterward, Mom let us shower and then called Mathew in for his bath. She checked him too, finding a tiny red dot on his shoulder. When asked, Mathew said I hadn't done anything to him.

Later, Mom warned me not to tell anyone about what had happened or she'd make my life miserable. I didn't know who to trust—who could I tell without getting into trouble?

On Sunday, it was time to return to the Johnsons' house. I was surprisingly relieved to go back. Nagymama kissed me goodbye and asked what was wrong. I said nothing, but she could tell something was bothering me.

She asked Mom, "What's wrong with Maria? She's not herself. What did you do to her? She's changed after she had a shower on Friday. What did you do to her?"

Mom reassured her, "Nothing's wrong with her. I swear to God Mom, I did nothing wrong to her. She's just being difficult. Tell your grandmother everything is fine." I echoed Mom's words, said goodbye, and we left.

It's summertime, and we're spending most of our days by the pool. During this time, Mom gives up the apartment in Brooklyn and moves into a new place in New Jersey. One day, as Mathew walks barefoot on the concrete to the pool, Grandpa notices that he's limping.

"What's wrong, Mathew?" Grandpa asked.

"Nothing," Mathew replied.

"Come here, let me see." Grandpa examined his foot and discovered a splinter. "I can fix this, and it won't hurt, I promise."

"Really, it won't hurt at all?"

"Promise."

Grandpa went inside to get a needle and rubbing alcohol, then sat Mathew at the table in the backyard and removed the splinter.

Later that night, when Mom and Steve picked us up for the weekend, we had dinner at their house. Mom started examining Mathew's body and noticed a large water blister on the bottom of his foot—exactly where the splinter had been. Sarah and I tried to explain, but Mom didn't believe us.

Mom took me downstairs to meet the Italian lady who owned the catering trucks that served our apartment building. She introduced me to her and her daughter, who seemed nice but gave me an uneasy feeling. Mom bought cigarettes from the truck, and we headed back upstairs.

Mom told me that she'd be going to work with Steve and warned me to watch my back because she suspected I was up to my old "demonic ways." My heart just sank; I was unsure of what to do or say.

On Monday, I asked Steve if he knew what Mom accused me of doing to my siblings.

"Oh yeah, she thinks you're hurting your sister and brother," he says.

"Then why don't you tell her it's not true?"

"I've tried, Maria, but she doesn't believe me no matter how many times I say it."

When we returned home, Nagymama was still at our apartment but wanted to go back to Brooklyn. Steve asked if she could wait until tomorrow so he could take her and us home, and she agreed. Mom wanted us to stay longer, but I said I had a doctor's appointment.

The next day, when we got back to the Johnsons', I told Karen that Mom had been acting strangely, accusing me of harming the kids and being a "devil worshiper." Karen told the social worker but didn't inform Mom. The social worker went to court with Mom again, and although visitation weekends were extended, we were not returned to her immediately.

As weekends went by, Karen also started acting weird. I told her about Mom's accusations, but Karen told me to stop exaggerating. One weekend, Mom locked me in my room and demanded that I admit to being a devil worshiper. I refused, and eventually, Mom took me out and said we were going for a car ride.

We ended up at Aunt Paula's apartment on 96th Street and the FDR. I was relieved to see them, hoping Aunt Paula could reason with Mom. However, Mom never let me talk to her alone.

The weekend ended, and it was time to return to Karen's house. Karen told Sarah to go downstairs first while she kept me behind.

"What's up?" I asked.

"Nothing," Karen replied. "You're just not going to be torturing your sister."

"What are you talking about?"

"Your mother told me you're torturing your siblings."

"That's not true? How can you believe her? She's mentally ill."

"I don't think so, Maria. I think she's trying to protect her younger children from you."

"Oh my God, I can't believe you. You're making my life a nightmare."

When we returned, Nagymama was still at the apartment, which was a relief. We had dinner together, and I helped with the dishes. Afterward, I stayed in the kitchen to paint the window sills. We were still working on the apartment, and it needed to be finished before school started.

Mom told me the apartment had been blessed by Nagymama, so none of my "demonic powers" would work inside the house. I teared up at her words, but she warned, "Don't you dare cry, or I'll burn out your eye sockets."

I ran into the bathroom and locked myself in. Nagymama asked what was wrong, but I lied, saying nothing, because I was scared of what might happen.

12

The judge granted custody to my mom. We were all crying at the Johnsons' entrance as we left their home. I cried because I knew I was in serious trouble with my mother, no matter what I did. I started middle school in New Jersey, and my mom began working downstairs with the Italian lady from the catering trucks.

One weekend, as I was taking a bath, my mom burst into the bathroom, pulled my hair, and slapped me. She told me not to cry.

"Don't you dare cry. You know what you did."

I protested, "I didn't do anything."

"Yes, you did," she insisted. "You keep doing things to the kids. Mathew doesn't want to eat his breakfast because you're sending him your demonic powers so he starves to death. I will kill you before that ever happens. Do you understand?"

I answered, "Yes."

The next day, our old social worker came over for a house visit disguised as a dinner. My mom wouldn't let me be alone in the dining room with him, fearing I might tell him about her behavior. After he left, I wished he had stayed longer. As soon as he was gone, my mom started yelling at me. "I saw you trying to give him messages telepathically. Get in the bathroom."

Once I was in the bathroom, she slapped me and yanked my hair.

"If you try that again, I'm going to kill you. Do you understand?"

I replied, "Yes, I understand."

Then, she followed me to my room. "What are you doing with your stepfather?" she demanded.

"Nothing," I said.

"You better not be doing anything with him, or I will kill you."

The next day, instead of going to school, I used my bus pass to travel to New York City. I went to Aunt Paula's apartment and told her about the crazy things happening at home. Aunt Paula couldn't believe it and said she had to call my mother. I begged her not to, explaining that my mom keeps accusing me of harming the kids and blaming it on my so-called demonic powers.

I said, "What is wrong with her? I can't escape her, and everyone seems to take her side. Aunt Paula, we went to an ice cream parlor in New Jersey where a song by Pat Benatar called 'Hell Is for Children' was playing. She claimed I made the song with my demonic powers. What the hell is wrong with her, not me? She needs to be back in the loony bin. I can't live with her. She keeps saying she's going to kill me one day for hurting the kids. I've never done anything to the kids."

Despite my pleas, Aunt Paula called my mom. The next day, my stepfather, mother, and siblings came to pick me up. My mom started kissing and hugging me. When we got home, she told me I was not allowed to run away again. I asked why she bothered coming for me if she hated me anyway. She said that wasn't true and that I was making things up.

The following afternoon, while getting up from the sofa, I fell to the floor. My kneecap had dislocated again, just like it had at the Johnsons' house, but Karen wasn't there to help. I screamed as my mom rushed over.

"What happened?" she asked. I explained that my kneecap had shifted to the back of my leg, causing my thigh and leg to go in different directions.

The ambulance arrived and secured my leg to a frame to prevent further displacement. I screamed throughout the ride to the hospital, apologizing to everyone in the ambulance.

At the hospital, two doctors worked on me. One pulled my leg one way while the other manipulated my kneecap. The pain was excruciating as my leg was realigned. The doctor decided I needed a cast to keep my leg immobile for proper healing. When we got home, I looked at the stairs leading up to our apartment on the second floor, a daunting fifteen steps. Climbing them was a hellish ordeal, but I managed to make it up.

"You can't go to school with that cast on, at least not yet," my mom said. "I'll pick up your schoolwork, and you can do it at home until you get better."

The first day after the cast was put on, my mom came upstairs and said, "I hear you. I can only come so fast."

"What, Mom?"

"You. You were knocking."

"No, Mom, I wasn't knocking."

"Well, your sister isn't here; she's at school. So, it has to be you. Don't tell me it wasn't you. Why are you knocking on the floor when you know I'm busy working? What's wrong with you?"

"Nothing, Mom, I'm not knocking."

"So, I'm making this up? Do you think I enjoy going up and down these stairs? Try it again and see what happens."

She came upstairs with lunch, and I couldn't get off the sofa fast enough to hide in the bathroom before she grabbed me by the hair. She yanked me back to the sofa and told me to act natural.

The Italian lady from downstairs came to check on me since the fall. She told me I looked well. A week later, my mom decided I was ready to go back to school. She sent me off and instructed me to come straight home because I was going to work with her and the Italian lady.

When I got home, I went straight downstairs to work. I cracked eggs, mixed them with an electric mixer, and helped make sandwiches. After finishing work, we went back upstairs. My mom made Italian sausages, which I detest because they have fennel seeds. She made me eat them while yelling at me the entire time. Then, she started yelling at Steve for his music, telling him to turn it off. He refused. Their argument escalated, and they both grabbed a knife and started wrestling with it. I was terrified and intervened, but things didn't end well for me. I ended up with a deep cut on my hand. My mom apologized and they made up.

A week later, my mom told Sarah it wasn't my fault that I was bad; I was born this way. She asked Sarah why she thought I did bad things. When Mom came back to me, she said Sarah had spared me and said nothing. Mom also said she didn't believe Sarah or Mathew and that I needed an exorcism. I wondered how I was going to get out of this situation this time.

The next morning, just as I was about to leave for school, my mom told me she was taking me to church instead. Just the two of us. She gave me a strange look. I left the house and, as before, took a bus down the road, then another to New York City, and finally a bus to Upstate New York where my Uncle Luis's family lives with Aunt Irene. My Aunt Maria took Sarah and me to stay with her before when we were hiding from Carlos. Maybe I could hide out in her apartment again.

When I arrived at Aunt Irene's apartment, she noticed my condition and asked, "Maria, what happened to you? You look awful."

"The cast is from my kneecap dislocating. The cut on my hand is from the knife when my parents were fighting. The bruise on my face is from my mom hitting me and telling the Italian lady downstairs it's from me falling. I told the foster mother, Karen, about her, but she didn't believe me. I told Aunt Paula, and she sent me back to her. My grandmother is too old and sick to care for us, and they won't give her custody. Aunt Maria put us in foster care. It feels like I'm cursed and I don't know what to do."

She was listening to me. When I finished, she went on to call somebody.

"Aunt Irene, what are you doing?" I asked.

"I'm calling your Uncle Luis."

"Why?"

"Because he might know what to do."

Aunt Irene called Uncle Luis, saying she had someone who

needed his help.

"Really? Who? "Maria? She left me a long time ago."

"No, not your wife Maria. Little Maria."

"Really? What happened?"

Aunt Irene explained everything, but Uncle Luis said he couldn't do anything for me. Aunt Irene said I could stay, but only for the night. I spent the entire day vomiting. I asked Aunt Irene if I could stay another day or two. She agreed but asked for my mom's phone number. I gave her the Italian lady's number since we didn't have a phone. Aunt Irene called and informed my mom that I was there and safe. My mom said they would come for me another day.

My mom and Steve came to Aunt Irene's place and they picked me up. As soon as I got into the car, my mother hit me on the head with a hairbrush. The next day, she told me that my demonic ways had to change. She started accusing Steve of sleeping with me and he denied it so she began throwing his stereo equipment down the stairs.

The guys that lived next door called the police on my parents. Now that Steve was gone, my mom was now focused on me.

"You whore... I told you to not fuck around, didn't I," she came into my room and started beating me up. She punched me in the face, in the belly. Then she told me to get into the other room; the room that belonged to my little sister and brother and she locked me inside the room. Then she came back into the room and bit me on my forehead and punched me in the face and then the belly.

"Do you want to fuck? Fuck me like you did Steve."

"No, no, no, get off, please mom."

She left again. Again, she came in, slapped me, and said, "I'm going to bring you your demonic shoes and you are going to leave this house and you are not going to look back because if you look back, I'm going to take this big knife, do you see this knife, Maria, I'm going to have to kill your sister and brother with the knife... Do you understand? Here is your demonic money and now get the fuck out of here, you demon."

I boarded the first bus to New York City and met my stepfather at his job. He gave me some money and instructed me to go to my grandfather's house in New Jersey. Fortunately, it was in a completely different part of the state. When I arrived at my grandfather's house, he was furious. He wanted to know what had been happening with my mother.

I explained that she hadn't been taking her medications and believed I was possessed by the devil. My Nagypapa, always so kind and understanding, told me that she had been this way since meeting my father and started using illegal drugs instead of taking her prescribed medications. He took me to food shopping and made me dinner.

A couple of days later, my former social worker arrived at my grandfather's house to pick me up and take me to where the other kids were. They drove me to the home of an Italian lady I didn't know, all the way in Upstate New York. She and her mother were very sweet, spending their time cooking and sewing our clothes. When Sarah first saw me, she was frightened by my appearance. Mathew, however, just asked if I was okay. I said yes, and that was all he seemed to care about.

Derrick arrived to take us back to stay with him and Karen. When he first saw me, he was shocked by my condition. He then asked why I hadn't called, and I explained, "Why would I call when Karen doesn't believe me?"

"What do you mean?" Derrick asked.

"I told her that my mom was acting strangely and accusing me of things I didn't do. Karen took my mom's side, so why would I trust you? I can't rely on you."

Derrick assured me that I could trust him, though I was still wary of his wife. Karen had let me down by sending me back to my mother, showing that she didn't truly care about me. Derrick had come with their friend Marcia, who had about a dozen kids. I really liked Marcia; she was always friendly and had a warm smile.

Marcia had told Karen to not allow Donald to jump up and down and rub his body against my sister Sarah. Basically, he was humping her like a dog. Donald was a freaking animal and I hated him. He was a pervert and he was mean to me and played too rough with Mathew.

We were now on our way back to the Johnsons house but I had told Derrick this time that I didn't want Donald in my room no matter what.

"I don't want him touching my sister no matter what. I also don't want him being too rough with Mathew or I would tell the social worker. I'm tired of people messing with me, my sister, and my brother and I really mean it."

I was crying but Derrick knew that I meant every word that I said. Marcia told Derrick about Donald humping Sarah. She told him about bringing it to Karen's attention and I had thanked her that day. She had asked me why. I had told her because I had told Karen and she just kept on telling me to stop complaining. Now Derrick knew that Karen was defending his son Donald too much and that he was out of control. He also knew that Karen was aware of my mom's condition before she got custody of us kids. He knew that she should have said something to the social worker and not allowed us to go and live with my mother.

Derrick promised things would be different this time. We finished our coffee and cake that these beautiful Italian ladies had given us. We hugged and thanked them for sewing the holes in our clothes and cooking all the yummy cakes and cookies for us. They really were very nice to us every day. They would cook elaborate Italian meals from scratch and they would launder our clothes. The grandmother in the house would always hug and kiss Mathew. She really liked him.

We got into Derrick's car with Derrick and Marcia and we were on our way back to the Johnsons. It took us four hours to get home. Finally, I said we were home and Mathew ran out of the car. He was the first at the door. I was the last to walk in. Everyone was happy to see us and started to give Sarah and Mathew hugs and kisses. Then everyone saw me.

Jenny said, "Maria, what happened to your face?"

"Oh my God..." said Peggy, "Mom said your mother hit you, but that's not hitting. You look like a truck ran you over and a wild animal bit you on your forehead. Why did she bite you? Who does that, is she crazy?"

Then Mike said, "I'm sorry your mom hit you, but I'm glad you're back here."

Then this new kid who looked like he was on fire said to me, "Wow... You really got the shit kicked out of you."

I couldn't help but start crying again, and Karen came over, trying to give me a hug. I pulled away and said, "No, you let me go back to her. It's your fault."

Karen responded, "Maria, I truly thought your mom was telling me the truth. I didn't realize she was that sick and making everything up. I promise I won't let her hurt you again. I promise, Maria. I love you. I know you think I don't care, but I really do."

"Okay," I said, "please don't let her in this house anymore. She wants to kill me! She keeps saying I'm possessed by the devil. She is absolutely crazy. I don't want her anywhere near me, no matter what Sarah or Mathew want. They always want to be with her because they don't get the shit kicked out of them."

"No, Maria, don't be scared. You're safe here. Everyone knows to call the police if your mother shows up. I promise."

"Okay, I'm just scared and tired. I want to be left alone."

I then turned to the burnt-looking kid in the corner. "Who are you?" I asked.

He replied, "My name is Sam."

"When did you get here?"

"Just last week."

"How long were you guys here before?"

"We were here for almost two years."

Jenny then said, "Come upstairs to my room, Maria."

"Okay," I said, "sorry, we'll talk later."

In Jenny and Peggy's room, which had small rosebud wallpaper and light pink carpet, Jenny put on Def Leppard music and told me they missed me and Sarah. They were curious about my school in New Jersey. I explained that between running away, being beaten, and having my leg in a cast, I was hardly in school. For the brief time I was there, the school seemed much like the one here. The only thing I liked about New Jersey was the catering shop downstairs. It kept my mom away from me most of the time, and they made great food. I enjoyed their macaroni salad, egg sandwiches, and meatball heroes. I even learned to crack eggs with both hands at the same time.

Peggy didn't quite believe me, but Jenny said, "I believe you, Maria. You've always been good at cooking, like when you did extra credit in home economics and made cookies and muffins."

Peggy then asked, "How have things been here?"

Jenny replied, "The same as usual."

"What about the new boy, Sam? He seems different."

"He was in a fire when he was little, and they keep doing surgery to try to make him look normal."

"Yeah, but he's scary-looking. Not to be mean, but he kind of scared me for a minute."

"It took us a day or so to get used to how he looks."

"Maria, come here," Karen called. I went to her room, where she was with her friend Marcia.

"Take off those sweatpants and try these on," Karen said.

I struggled with the pants because of my cast. "I can't get them all the way on."

"Here, let me help," Karen said, and she assisted me. "Don't worry, I'm going to call the doctor on Monday morning to have the cast removed. For now, here are some other pants and a couple of tops."

"Thanks," I said. "I really appreciate it."

Karen responded, "I understand what it's like to be the oldest and have so much responsibility while making do without because the younger ones come first."

"Right," I agreed. "Thanks."

I asked Jenny to help me take my new clothes down to my room in the basement, as I couldn't hold onto the railings with the clothes in my hands.

I reached the bottom of the stairs in the basement and saw that my bed was in place. However, the room had changed: there was now carpeting on the floor and a panel wall behind my dresser. I went over to the panel wall and noticed that it separated the girls' space—Sarah's and mine—from the boys' area, which now included Mike, Mathew, and the new kid, Sam.

Jenny said, "Mom had your room fixed up before you guys got here as a surprise. Do you like it?"

"Yeah," I replied. "The floor here is always too cold, so I love having carpet. I especially like the panel wall; it gives us a little privacy. We won't see Mike when he's changing his clothes."

Karen, who had been behind me on the steps, asked, "Mike used to change his clothes in front of you girls?"

"Not directly in front of us, but on his and Mathew's side of the room."

"Where do you girls change?"

"I almost always change inside the walk-in closet. If not, I use the bathroom upstairs when I'm getting ready for school. It's just easier to get dressed and wash up in the bathroom; it saves time. Sarah changes out here in the room, out in the open, but now that she's getting a bit older, she should follow my lead and be more respectful of her privacy."

Karen nodded. "Yes, I'm going to talk with her. She's still little and doesn't fully understand; her mind is too innocent. Mike, on the other hand, is a different story. I'm going to have a serious talk with him. He is not allowed to get undressed in front of you girls, no matter what. If he does that again, you let me know."

"Okay," I said. "And thank you for the carpet and the privacy."

"You're welcome," Karen replied. "Welcome home."

13

The cast came off, and I returned to school for the second time. I reconnected with my friends Jennifer and Jackie, and seventh grade was shaping up to be a lot of fun. We had home economics, where we learned to cook and use a sewing machine. When the quarter ended, we started art class, but this time it was pottery. I loved the pottery wheel; it was challenging to keep my hands steady while it spun, but it was rewarding once I got the hang of it. I was making an ashtray for Mother's Day for Karen. I thought she'd like it because it's not plain and ugly like the ones she and Derrick use. This one will have flowers and different colors, so it'll be very pretty.

At lunchtime, I visited the guidance counselor, who told me I needed to see the school psychologist during my study hall period. I asked why. She said it was to help me work through my feelings because of what I had experienced in the past. I was confused. Why did I need to see a psychologist just because I asked to be moved out of Mrs. Rubik's class? I had told her that my foster brother claimed Mrs. Rubik's husband was a Satanist, that it was his religion and he wore a ring to show it. I was scared because of all the crazy stuff I had been through with my parents. My biological father, Carlos, took my little sister Sarah and me, at ages six and nine, to watch *The Exorcist* at a drive-in theater with the speaker inside the car. Then my schizophrenic mother constantly told me I was possessed by the devil and that I deserved to die because I belonged in hell.

"Why do I have to be punished?" I asked.

"You're not being punished. We just want to make sure that everything you've gone through hasn't negatively affected you. It's good to talk about your feelings, especially when you're angry. Your teachers have said that you seem angry all the time and you don't want to participate in class. Why is that, Maria?"

"No reason."

"Maria, you need to see the school psychologist starting tomorrow."

"Okay, I'll go."

The next day, I met Dr. Smith, the school psychologist.

"How are you, Maria? You must be Maria?"

"Yes, I'm fine now. Can I leave?"

"No, you cannot leave. You need to participate in the conversation with me. I want to understand why you're so angry all the time. Your teachers say you're angry."

"I don't want to talk about it. Nothing will change. I'm stuck where I am, and that bitch is in control. There's always someone making my life a living hell, and I can't do anything about it. Adults twist words to make things look how they want them to and make us kids look wrong, so forget it."

"Like what, Maria?"

"Nothing."

"Do you sleep well, Maria?"

"No!"

"Why not?"

"What do you mean, why not? Who can sleep when your

siblings are asking the social worker to send us back to my crazy schizophrenic mother? Then my foster mother is always yelling at my little brother to eat. And my foster brother plays too rough with him. One day, he's going to break something on my little brother. Karen doesn't say anything because he's her real son. She didn't say anything about him humping my little sister either. I told her that Mike had come to my bed and touched me. She asked him if it was true, and he said no. Then she told me to stop making up stories. Her son and the boys can do whatever they want.

One of the boys pushed me into the walk-in closet and pushed me to the ground. He closed the door behind him. Karen had taken Sarah shopping with her along with Peggey. Jenny was at soccer practice; Derrick was at work. I was alone on the floor of the closet with this jerk. I tried to get up. He kicked me down again and laughed at me and said 'Who's going to help you? No one is here, and no one is going to believe you anyway.' He had one leg on my belly holding me down. Then he unzipped his pants and took out his penis, he said suck it. I said no to him and he hit me. When Karen got home, I told her about it and she told me to stop making up stories.

So sorry if this sounds petty but people always say that we kids complain about the obvious chores so here goes, Sarah, Peggy, and I do most of the chores in the house. The laundry, cooking, raking the dog poop and the leaves, and cleaning our rooms. We also have to go with Karen to clean houses except for Sarah, she's still too little. We have to clean the houses with bleach. So that Karen can rent them out, and she gives us ten freaking dollars in the entire MONTH for this! I do earn money on the side babysitting Mike's niece. His older brother has this beautiful little girl with his girlfriend. Whenever they need a babysitter, they call me. Tom, Mike's older brother, did offer me pot once when I was babysitting. He said that he offered it to Jenny and she liked it. It figures Jenny would smoke pot, what an airhead. I told him sorry but I'm not a fucking drug addict, and he got pissed off but I didn't care."

Dr. Smith was listening to me calmly. Then he said, "Maria, have you said anything to your social worker?"

"Yes, and Karen spoke with him and convinced him that I was making it all up or exaggerating. So now you tell me, how am I supposed to sleep well?"

"You can go to Class Maria. I will see you the day after tomorrow."

****

"Hello Mr. Davis (the social worker), how are you?"

"I'm fine Maria, how are you doing?"

"Is it more important?"

"Oh... I'm just peachy. Mr. Smith tells me there are issues at home that I'm not aware of."

"Really, I thought you already knew. I told you that he pushed me to the ground and he told me to suck it and Karen is defending him. I heard the conversation she had with you on the phone. She said it's her word against his and there's no way to prove what she's saying is true. Did you know that these people are also prejudiced?"

"No, I don't think that's possible."

"Really, then why did their son, their biological son Donald, call me a SPICK?"

"He called you a Spick, I can't believe that."

"He said that since we are half Puerto Rican, we are half Spick."

"Oh..."

"And because my brother Mathew is from a different father, he isn't my full brother. Why don't you believe me? Just because I'm a kid and she's a parent doesn't make her right and me wrong. She's also never home. In the evenings, they go to their friends' homes or out line dancing and talk about us kids. I know because when it's their turn, their friends come over and all they do is talk about us kids. What we do, say, eat, play, dress, grades, sports, dance, and anything else you can think of. I hear it because I'm at the bottom of the stairs so I hear everything.

Karen takes me to clean houses with bleach when she knows I have asthma. She put straight bleach on the floor last weekend and I started wheezing. She came outside and told me to stop faking it. That bitch is just as crazy as the fucking schizophrenic mother that I have. On top of that, she wants me and Sarah on diets but she keeps telling us we have to make pasta for dinner. Pasta is fattening for dinner. It's only good for runners. Do I look like I want to run track? No... Even Jenny, who I thought I was close with, is changing the way she looks at people.

It was after my thirteenth birthday and I said to Jenny that there were these two new kids in school. The two kids are sister and brother related but they kind of stick out at our school. Why do they stick out at your school? The schools out there aren't the same as out here in New York City. Here in New York, there is everybody, black, white, brown, Asian, Hispanic.

So far there have only been white and very few Spanish. The few Spanish are part white like Sarah and me. These two kids are black and Jenny keeps saying that the girl smells. I asked her why she smells, is it from running or going to the gym? She said, no she just stinks. You know how Niggers are. I said to her no I don't know how they are. I have had black friends in school and they were just as nice as the white and the Spanish. Then she takes out harlequin novels and reads the dirty passages to my little sister. When I told Karen, she brought out another book and says I'm lying. Everyone in that house is always lying."

"Okay Maria, I will look into it. By the way, the court is coming up soon and you have to speak to the judge about wanting to go home with your mother."

"What are you crazy about now? Get the fuck out of here, I've had enough. I'm taking the train back home and I don't want to be bothered."

****

"Hello Reverend, how are you?"

"Fine... Glad you could join us, Maria, on this lovely day."

"Do I have a choice?"

"Sure, you do... You could be locked away in punishment for reflection time, or in a straight jacket, or be heavily medicated, or any number of other options."

"Nice... So I'm being punished because I don't want to live anymore. Isn't being stuck in this mental hospital for kids enough? Why can't you people just let me drop dead already, I'm so fucking fed up with everything and everyone."

"Maria, what do you like?"

"I like to cook with my Nagymama. I like the sound of my brother's laughter. I like how silly and funny Sarah is."

"Now, Maria if you were gone, don't you think that they would miss you?"

"Yes, but it would be just for a little while and then their lives would go on. My pain would stop. I wouldn't have to worry about him coming to my bed at night when everyone's asleep. I wouldn't have to fight for basic rights inside the house I live in. I wouldn't have to fight for respect or for them to stop bothering my siblings or calling me names. Karen constantly telling me that I'm fat or her son calling me lard ass. I wouldn't have to feel like a minority or less of a person. I'm tired of fighting. What should I do? I don't want to go back to living with my mother, but Sarah and Mathew do and they don't know how dangerous it is to be with her."

"Maria, why don't you ask to be removed?"

"Removed from where?"

"Your current home has to be rehomed someplace else. It sounds like you need to be someplace else for your well-being."

"Okay, but what about my little sister and brother?"

"What about them?"

'Can they come with me?"

"Most likely not... But I will ask your caseworker for you."

"Mr. Davis, I didn't know you would come and visit me in the crazy hospital."

"Maria, why did you try to kill yourself?"

"Because it seems like my only way out of this nightmare. I'm tired of people, boys touching me, even the nice one I thought, John, touched my private parts underneath the blanket on the sofa when we were watching television and his mother Karen was lying down on the sofa. I had a blanket on me because it was cold so did Karen. John came and sat next to me like usual but this time he took some of the blanket. I didn't think anything of him taking part of the blanket because he's done that before and nothing's happened. This time was different, he put his hand on my private parts and I moved it away. He put his hand back again so I took the remote and pretended that I accidentally threw it on his private.

I've had enough of those fucked up people, that you think are nice. They are only nice when you look at them but watch out when the lights are off. Derrick is the only nice one but he's never home. Derrick is always working. We have lots of fun with Derrick at the beach or in the pool. He dunks us or throws us in the water but in a fun way and he's never been fresh to me. He's the only one and my little brother and that kid Sam are the only ones that have never been fresh to me. The other boys have done things and made me do things. I'm not a virgin you know but you keep on thinking that the bitch Karen is a great mom. She should get a Nobel Peace Prize."

"Maria, we think you could benefit from being placed in a different home."

"Can you make it so my little sister and brother can come with me?"

"I will try but it's very hard Maria, placing a child let alone three but I will see what I can do. In the meantime, you will be going home tomorrow. Please don't do anything to yourself, promise?"

"Yeah, okay."

****

"I'm leaving for religion class. I'll be back later," I told Karen. She asked me to get home right after.

"What else am I going to do? It's dark out there."

Kevin is in my class from school. I'm surprised he's not locking lips with some girl in here like he does in school. We are sitting at the same long table so we're in the same religion class. The Nun comes over and tells me you have a beautiful name. I said 'Thank you.' She asked each of us why we wanted to do our confirmation and we each had different answers.

Kevin asks if he can walk me home. I said it's a free country but don't try anything. He said like what?

"Like kissing me, don't try and kiss me or I will belt you one."

"No, I wasn't going to. I was going to ask you can we do our science project together during study hall?"

"Yeah... Okay, but you're going to actually do some work and not think that I am going to do all of the work, understand?"

"Got it. I will see you tomorrow."

"Maria, why did you break Mike's record? He asked.

"Because he's a pervert and he needs to keep his hands to himself. Now what? I woke up last night and he was touching me but he sneaked out today to go to the city to see his social worker so I broke his record because I couldn't punch him in the face."

The next day in the evening, the police showed up at the house and told Derrick and Karen that Mike and his friend had been impersonating a police officer.

When Mike got home that night, Karen and Derrick asked Mike, "What have you been doing?"

"Nothing, just hanging out with Tom."

"Doing what?"

"Nothing."

He tries to go downstairs and Karen says, "Not so fast. The police were here. You and your friend have been impersonating a police officer. What do you have to say for yourself?"

"We didn't mean anything by it besides, it was Tom's fault. He said the girl would know that we were not real cops and she wouldn't say anything."

"Well, you're wrong and you're lucky that they don't come here and hall you off to jail. Especially since it was a woman, she could have felt in danger with you two men. Maria is probably right, there is something wrong with you. Go to your room, you're not allowed to hang out with Tom anymore. I don't want to hear anything about it and you're grounded.

Tomorrow you're going to wash my car and Dad's car. You will wax dad's car and you will cut the grass and do all the raking as well. That's to start and we're being nice because if this was John or Donald, they would have gotten a beating. Do you understand what we're saying to you?"

"Yes."

****

We are now in study hall trying to do our science project about the heart. I told Kevin I don't understand how we can make this interesting. Only old people want to hear about how the heart works or what's wrong with it. Kevin says maybe we can make a rhyme that sounds funny but that's also informative.

"Okay smarty, that sounds like a plan," I appreciated his idea.

Jackie and Jennifer came over and asked, "Are you going on the trip to Washington D.C.?"

"Of course, I'm going, I can't wait, it's going to be a lot of fun. I've never been to D.C. before... I heard there are so many things to see over there. It's going to be exciting."

"How are you getting to school that morning? Who's picking you up to take you back home?"

"I'm getting a ride with Nancy's mom coming to school and my dad Derrick said he will pick us up and bring us back."

"I can't believe we have to be here at four o'clock in the morning. Jennifer, I'm sitting with you, okay?"

"Great Maria, my mom packed extra snacks so we can share."

"Oh... thank you, Jennifer, your mom is so nice. My mom Karen never thinks about those things. My mom Lily had to beg her to give me twenty dollars so I would have money to buy food on the trip."

"You're supposed to have money to buy food, the teachers said for three meals and if you want souvenirs."

"I know but she doesn't care, she only cares about her boys and money."

"Yes, my mom Lily has to mail the twenty dollars to reimburse her the twenty dollars she gave me last night. Meanwhile, the foster agency would give her the money if she puts it on the expense report that she sends in every month."

"Expense Report?"

"Yeah, it's what they send in when they want to get money back for spending money on us kids. When we first moved in, she got us haircuts. They paid her back for that. She bought us school supplies and they paid her back. She put carpet in my room. They paid her back for that too."

I heard Karen talking to her friend Marcia, you know the one with the million kids. Well, a couple of them are going away to college. Karen was telling her how she could make money by taking in foster kids and not having to pay for anything. I heard her say that they even pay for the paper plates that we use for dinner. Look at the cherry blossom trees. They are beautiful. That is John Wilke's Booth. This is the Constitution of The United States of America. Tomorrow we will see the Lincoln Memorial."

Mrs. Rodriguez and Mr. Bentise are in the pool.

"Maria, are you coming?"

"No, I can't go."

"Why not Maria, I will wait until you put on your bathing suit."

"I got my period so I can't go in the pool."

"Okay Maria, sorry I will see you later then."

"Okay, later."

****

"Dad, everything was great but I'm hungry and I'm tired."

"Why are you hungry?"

"Because twenty dollars isn't enough for three meals."

"Three meals?"

"Yes Dad, three meals."

"Your mother never said anything about three meals."

"Yeah... I know... Can we just get home, please?

****

"So, what are you complaining about this time Maria?"

"Nothing."

"That's not what I heard. You know I could call up that hospital that you were in and tell them that you're not doing too well. This way they can take you back and you can stay there. The next time you tell your father that I did something, you better have something to back it up missy, you got that?"

"All I said was that twenty dollars is not enough for three meals."

"Maria, you probably misspent the money, that's why you didn't have enough."

"No, I bought lunch on the first day. The same on the second day. I only had two dollars left over for the third day. What was I supposed to do? I didn't ask anybody for anything,

122

all I did was stay on the bus.”

“You know Maria, I don’t like your attitude.”

“Well, I’m tired of living here. I think it’s time for me to go.”

****

“Mr. Davis, I can’t take it anymore.”

“Slow down Maria, why are you crying? Where are you calling from?”

“I’m calling from school. Karen said she was going to call the hospital and tell them that I wasn’t doing well so that they would take me back. She said this way I could stay there. I can’t live like this. I love my sister and brother but I can’t take it anymore. You gotta get me outta here please.”

“Yes, Maria, I will get you out of there just don’t do anything, please.”

“Okay, just get me out and tell her to stop her shit. Let her know that I spoke with you and that she can’t keep doing this.”

“Maria calm down, she doesn’t have the right to put you in the mental hospital just for no reason. I am going to talk to her and I am going to let her know that you will be leaving.”

****

“So, you spoke with Mr. Davis, you know you don’t have to leave this house. I wasn’t really going to put you back in the hospital.”

“Oh really, you just enjoy torturing me into thinking that you’re going to send me there whenever you want. I’ve had enough of you and this house."

Derrick walks in as we're shouting.

"What's going on?"

"I'm leaving and it's all her fault."

"My fault...? No Maria, it's up to you if you want to leave. This is still your home and you can stay."

"Oh yeah? Dad, she said she was going to put me back in the hospital."

"No Derrick, what I said was, I am worried about you and I don't want you to end back up in the hospital."

"She's lying, that's not what she said. Forget it, I'm done, I have to get out."

****

"Hello Mrs. Garcia, it's nice to meet you. I'm Maria and I was wondering how many children you have?"

"I have two... I have my son who goes to college and my daughter who is in her last year of high school."

"That's very nice."

"Maria, do you have any boyfriends?"

"No, and I don't want one either."

"What grade are you in now?"

"I'm in the eighth grade now. I just want to live in peace with no one to bother me. The house I am in has too many people and too many boys. The foster mother has boys sleeping in the same room as me and they are in high school. I don't want a boy sleeping in my room."

"Maria, come and look, this would be your room if you come and live with us. You will share it with my daughter Vicky. The room is pretty and I don't need much. I promise I won't be in any trouble."

The next day, I gave Sarah her Christmas gift and I left Mathew his Christmas gift with Sarah to give to him whenever she thought would be best. I know they probably will never forgive me for going to another family, but I can't think of dying as my only option.

Mr. Davis picked me up on December 5th, 1983, and took me with him to lunch before he dropped me off at Mrs. Garcia's home in New York City, where I became a part of the Garcia family for over forty years.

About the Author

Rose Calles, a first-generation American, was born and raised in the vibrant heart of New York City. With a Hungarian mother and a Puerto Rican father, Rose's upbringing was enriched by a unique blend of cultural traditions and values, grounded in Roman Catholic faith. This diverse heritage has greatly influenced her perspective and life's work. Rose holds a Bachelor's degree in Accounting and a Master's degree in Early Childhood Education and Special Education. Her academic background reflects her versatility, with a passion for both analytical precision and nurturing young learners.

Beyond her professional pursuits, Rose's greatest pride lies in her family. She is the proud mother of two accomplished adult children—her daughter holds two law degrees, and her son is excelling in Mechanical Engineering, having earned honors at the college level. Rose is also a devoted grandmother, and her granddaughter brings immeasurable joy and love into her life. For Rose, family is her most cherished accomplishment, providing a constant source of happiness, love, and comfort. Her story is a testament to the values of resilience, education, and the enduring power of family bonds.

Acknowledgments

<table>
<tr><td align="center"><u>National Runaway Safeline</u></td></tr>
<tr><td>Website:

https://www.1800runaway.org/youth-teens</td></tr>
<tr><td>Description:

A free, 24/7, confidential, and anonymous communications system for runaways, homeless youth, and their families. You can call 1-800-RUNAWAY (1-800-786-2929) or message the Safeline for help finding shelter, support, or just to talk. The Safeline can also help parents and guardians figure out next steps, such as contacting friends, family, or law enforcement.</td></tr>
</table>

<table>
<tr><td align="center"><u>Crisis Text Line</u></td></tr>
<tr><td>Website:

https://www.crisistextline.org/</td></tr>
<tr><td>Description:

Crisis Text Line provides free, 24/7, high-quality text-based mental health support and crisis intervention by empowering a community of trained volunteers to support people in their moments of need.</td></tr>
</table>

SAMHSA – Substance Abuse and Mental Health Services Administration (.gov)
Website: https://www.samhsa.gov/find-help
Description: SAMHSA's mission is to lead public health and service delivery efforts that promote mental health, prevent substance misuse, and provide treatments and supports to foster recovery while ensuring equitable access and better outcomes.

AdoptUSKids
Website: https://www.adoptuskids.org/
Description: AdoptUSKids educates families about foster care and adoption and gives child welfare professionals information and support to help them improve their services. We also maintain the nation's only federally funded photolisting service that connects waiting children with families.

References

Songs

- Kung Fu Fighting by Carlton George Douglas, 1974

- The Bottle by Brian Jackson and Gil Scott-Heron, 1974

- Mercy Mercy Me (The Ecology), What's Going On Album by Marvin Gaye, 1971

- Ngiculela-Es Una Historia-I am by Stevie Wonder, Songs in the Key of Life, 1976

- Black Magic Woman/ Oye Como Va and Sa A Cabo by Carlos Santana's Abraxas's album, 1970

- Instant Replay by Dan Hartman, 1978

- In The Bush by Musique, 1978

- Hot Shot by Karen Young, 1978

- YMCA by The Village People J, 1978

- Another One Bites The Dust by Queen, 1980

- Rapper's Delight by The Sugarhill Gang, 1980

- Special Lady by Ray Goodman and Brown, 1980

- The Beat Goes On by Whispers, 1980

- Let's Get Serious by Jermaine Jackson, 1980

- Take Your Time by SOS Band, 1980

- The Star-Spangled Banner by Donna Summer, 1978

- The Jackson 5, 1978

- Hell is for Children by Pat Benatar, 1980

- Blondie, Johann Sebastian Bach, Saturday Night Fever Album, 1977 (References to the Bee Gees and John Travolta)

<u>TV Shows or Movies</u>

- The Love Boat
- The Wizard of Oz
- The Exorcist (1973)
- All My Children
- General Hospital
- Star Wars R2D2 and C-3PO (1977)

<u>Places</u>

- New York City East 96th Street and The FDR
- Brooklyn Graham Avenue Williamsburg
- Queens
- Bronx
- Parkchester
- New Jersey
- Colorforms Toy

www.ingramcontent.com/pod-product-compliance
Lightning Source LLC
Chambersburg PA
CBHW071337150726
47997CB00002B/760